A COMPLETE GUIDE TO THE DIVINE LITURGY

A Step-by-Step Guide to the Orthodox Liturgy of Saint John Chrysostom

Authored & Compiled by:
Alexander Egger
Contributions by:
Fr. Antony Balnaves

Independently Published
by Nevsky Publications
- 2025 -

Nevsky Publications

Published by Nevsky Publications
Independent Researcher
ISBN: 9798336125474
www.nevskypublications.com
Copyright © 2025

All rights reserved under international copyright conventions. No part of this book may be reproduced or utilized in any manner in any form or by any means, whatsoever, including electronic or mechanical, including photocopying, scanning, recording, or by any information storage and retrieval system, without written permission except in the case of brief quotations embodied in critical articles and reviews.

This book is sold subject to the condition that it shall not, by way of trade or otherwise, be lent, re-sold, hired out, or otherwise circulated without the publisher's prior consent in any form of binding or cover other than in which it is published and without a similar condition including this condition imposed on the subsequent purchaser.

Scripture taken from the St. Athanasius Academy Septuagint™. Copyright © 2008 by St. Athanasius Academy of Orthodox Theology. Used by permission. All rights reserved.

Scripture taken from the New King James Version®. Copyright © 1982 by Thomas Nelson. Used by permission. All rights reserved.

This book's content is based on the version of The Divine Liturgy of Our Father Among the Saints John Chrysostom, published by Holy Trinity Monastery of ROCOR.

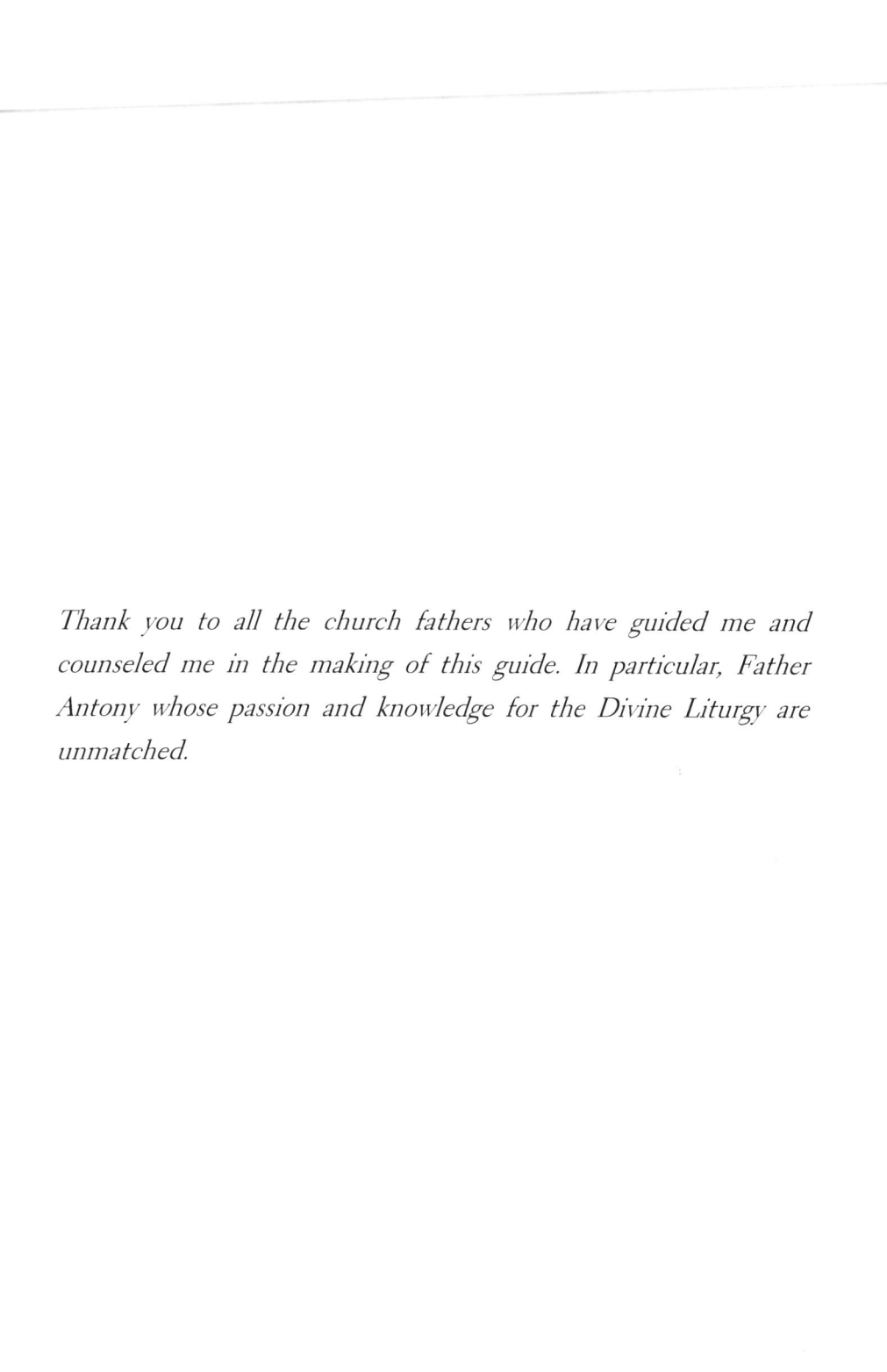

Thank you to all the church fathers who have guided me and counseled me in the making of this guide. In particular, Father Antony whose passion and knowledge for the Divine Liturgy are unmatched.

"The Divine Liturgy is the way we know God and the way God becomes known to us...Every Divine Liturgy is a Theophany. The Body of Christ appears. Every member of the Church is an icon of the Kingdom of God. After the Divine Liturgy we must continue to iconify the Kingdom of God, keeping His commandments. The glory of Christ is for Him to bear His fruit in every member."

- Elder Sophrony of Essex

Table of Contents

INTRODUCTION	1
THE PROSKOMEDIA	4
THE DIVINE LITURGY OF SAINT JOHN CHRYSOSTOM	9
THE GREAT LITANY	11
PRAYER OF THE FIRST ANTIPHON	21
THE FIRST ANTIPHON	23
FIRST SMALL LITANY	27
PRAYER OF THE SECOND ANTIPHON	29
THE SECOND ANTIPHON	31
THE SECOND SMALL LITANY	35
PRAYER OF THE THIRD ANTIPHON	37
THE THIRD ANTIPHON	39
THE SMALL ENTRANCE	41
THE TRISAGION HYMN	43
THE EPISTLE	50
PRAYER OF THE GOSPEL	52
THE HOLY GOSPEL	54
LITANY OF FERVENT SUPPLICATION	56
LITANY OF THE CATECHUMENS	59
THE LITURGY OF THE FAITHFUL	61
CHERUBIC HYMN	63
THE GREAT ENTRANCE	69
LITANY OF SUPPLICATION	75

PRAYER OF PREPARATION	85
THE CREED (SYMBOL OF FAITH)	89
THE HOLY ANAFORA	95
HYMN TO THE THEOTOKOS	111
THE LITANY BEFORE THE LORD'S PRAYER	121
THE LORD'S PRAYER	125
HOLY COMMUNION	131
THE COMMUNION HYMN	133
PRAYER OF THANKSGIVING	157
PRAYER BEFORE THE AMBO	161
REFERENCES & SOURCES	170

INTRODUCTION

IC XC
NI KA

The liturgy is the most important divine service. In it the most holy Mystery of Communion is celebrated, as established by our Lord Jesus Christ on Holy Thursday evening, the eve of His Passion. After giving praise to His heavenly Father, the Lord took bread, blessed it, and broke it, and gave it to the apostles, saying, "Take! Eat! This is My Body which is broken for you…" Then He took the cup of wine and blessed it and gave it to them with the words, "Drink ye all of it! For this is My Blood of the New Testament which is shed for many, for the forgiveness of sins." And when they had communed of these, the Lord gave them the commandment always to perform this Mystery, "Do this in remembrance of Me" (Matt. 26:26-28, Lk. 22:19; 1 Cor. 11:24).

The Apostles celebrated Holy Communion according to the commandment and example of Christ and taught their disciples and successors to perform this great and saving Mystery. In the earliest times the order and form of celebrating the Liturgy were transmitted orally, and all the prayers and sacred hymns were memorized. Eventually, written explanations of the Apostolic Liturgy began to appear. As time passed, new prayers, hymns, and sacred actions were added in various churches. The need arose to unify the existing orders of the Liturgy for the sake of harmony in their celebration. In the fourth century, when the persecutions of the Romans against Christians ended, it was possible to re-establish good order in the Church's inner life through the Ecumenical Councils.

St. Basil the Great wrote a form of the Liturgy for general use, then, somewhat later, St. John Chrysostom wrote a shorter version of St. Basil's Liturgy. These Liturgies were based on the most ancient Liturgy, attributed to St. James the Apostle, the first bishop of Jerusalem. St. Basil the Great, who reposed in 379 A.D., was archbishop of Caesarea in Cappadocia in Asia Minor. He is called "the Great" because of his great ascetic endeavors and his literary contribution to the Church of numerous prayers and ecclesiastical writings and rules. St. John Chrysostom was an archbishop of Constantinople. He was called "Chrysostom" (in Greek, "the golden tongued") for his unique rhetorical gifts with which he proclaimed the Word of God. Though he reposed in 407 A.D. in exile, many volumes of his sermons and letters remain to edify us spiritually.

The Liturgy is described by various terms. "Liturgy" itself comes from a Greek word meaning "common action or service" and signifies that the Mystery of Holy Communion is the reconciling sacrifice of God for the sins of the entire community of faithful, the living and the dead. Because the Mystery of Holy Communion is called "Evharistia" in Greek or "the Thanksgiving Sacrifice," the Liturgy is also called the Eucharist. It is also termed the Mystical Supper or the Lord's Supper since it reminds us of the Mystical Supper performed by Christ. In Apostolic times the Liturgy was referred to as "breaking bread" (Acts 2:46, cf. 1 Cor. 10:16). In the Liturgy the two earthly life and teachings of Jesus Christ, from His Nativity to His Ascension into Heaven, are recalled, as well as the benefits which He bestowed upon the earth for our salvation.

The order of the Liturgy is as follows. First, the elements for the Mystery are prepared, then the faithful are prepared for the

Mystery, and finally the very Mystery itself is celebrated and the faithful receive Communion. These three parts are called:

I) the **Proskomedia**

II) the **Liturgy of the Catechumens**

III) the **Liturgy of the Faithful**

Notes:

THE PROSKOMEDIA

IC XC
NI KA

Proskomedia is a Greek word meaning offering. The first part of the Liturgy derives its name from the early Christian custom of the people offering bread and wine and all else that was needed for the Liturgy. Therefore, each small loaf of the bread which is used in it is termed a "prosphora," another word meaning offering. This bread or prosphora must be leavened, pure, and made of wheat flour. The Lord Jesus Christ Himself, for the celebration of the Mystery of Holy Communion, used leavened, not unleavened bread, as is clear from the Greek word used in the New Testament. The prosphora must be round and formed in two parts, one above the other, as an image of the two natures of Jesus Christ, divine and human. On the flat surface of the upper part a seal of the Cross is impressed, and in the four sections thus formed are the initial Greek letters of the name of Jesus Christ, "IC XC," and the Greek word "NIKA," which mean together "Jesus Christ conquers."

The wine used in the Mystery must be red grape wine, as this color reminds us of the color of blood. The wine is mixed with water to remind us of the pierced side of the Savior from which flowed blood and water on the Cross. Five prosphoras are used in the Proskomedia to recall the five loaves with which Christ miraculously fed the five thousand, an event which gave Him the means to teach the people about spiritual nourishment, about the incorrupt, spiritual food which is bestowed in the Mystery of Holy Communion (John 6:22-58). One prosphora, known as the Lamb, is used for Holy Communion, in accordance with the words of the Apostle: "For we, being many, are one bread and one body, for we are all partakers of that one Bread" (1 Cor. 10: 17).

The Proskomedia is performed by the priest in a quiet voice at the Table of Preparation when the sanctuary is closed. During its celebration, the Third and Sixth Hours are read.

The priest takes the first prosphora and with a small spear makes the sign of the Cross over it three times, saying the words, "In remembrance of our Lord and God and Savior, Jesus Christ." The priest then cuts a cube out of the center of this prosphora with the spear (a small, wedge-shaped knife) and pronounces the words of the Prophet Isaiah: "He was oppressed, and He was afflicted, yet He opened not His mouth; He is brought as a lamb to the slaughter; and as 3 a sheep before her shearers is dumb, so He openeth not His mouth. He was taken from prison and from judgment; and who shall declare His generation? For He was cut off out of the land of the living; for the transgressions of My people was He stricken" (Is. 53:7-8). This cube-shaped portion of the prosphora, called the Lamb (John 1:29), is placed on the diskos, a metal plate. Then the priest cuts a cross in the bottom of the Lamb while saying the words, "Sacrificed is the Lamb of God, who taketh away the sins of the world, for the life of the world and its salvation." He then pierces the right side of the Lamb with the spear, saying the words of the Evangelist, "One of the soldiers with a spear pierced His side, and forthwith there came out blood and water. And he that saw it bore record, and his record is true" (John 19:34). In accordance with these words wine is poured into the chalice mixed with water. From the second prosphora, the priest cuts out one portion in honor of the Virgin Mary and places it on the right side of the Lamb on the diskos. From the third prosphora, which is called "that of the nine ranks," are taken nine portions in honor of the saints, John the Forerunner and Baptist, the prophets, the Apostles, the hierarchs, the martyrs, the monastic saints, the unmercenary physicians, the grandparents of Jesus, Joachim and Anna, the saint who is celebrated that day, the saint to whom the church is dedicated, and finally the saint who composed the liturgy being celebrated. These portions are placed on the left side the Lamb. From the fourth prosphora, portions are removed for the hierarchs, the priesthood, and all the living. From the fifth prosphora, portions are taken for those Orthodox Christians who have reposed.

Finally, portions are removed from those prosphoras donated by the faithful, as the names of the health and salvation of living and for the repose of the dead. All these portions are placed on the diskos below the Lamb.

At the end of the Proskomedia the priest covers the bread with a metal asterisk (star) and then covers the diskos and chalice with special veils, censes the diskos and the chalice and prays that the Lord bless the offered Gifts and remember those who have offered them and those for whom they are offered.

The sacred instruments used and actions performed in the Proskomedia have symbolic meanings. The diskos signifies the caves in Bethlehem and Golgotha; the star, the star of Bethlehem and the Cross; the veils, the swaddling clothes and the winding sheet at the tomb of the Savior; the chalice, the cup in which Jesus Christ sanctified the wine; the prepared Lamb, the judgment, passion, and death of Jesus Christ; and its piercing by the spear, the piercing of Christ's body by one of the soldiers. The arrangement of all the portions in a certain order on the diskos signifies the entire Kingdom of God, whose members consist of the Virgin Mary, the angels, all the holy men who have been pleasing to God, all the faithful Orthodox Christians, living and dead, and, in the center, its head, the Lord Himself, our Savior. The censing signifies the overshadowing by the Holy Spirit, whose grace is shared in the Mystery of Holy Communion.

Notes:

The Start of the Divine Liturgy

"Blessed is the kingdom of the Father and the Son and the Holy Spirit, now and forever and to the ages of ages."

The opening sentence of the Orthodox Divine Liturgy serves as a powerful declaration of faith. It marks the commencement of a sacred journey where prayers are not just requests, but also a profound proclamation of our unwavering belief in God's eternal beauty, the Holy Trinity—Father, Son, and Holy Spirit—and the everlasting nature of their presence. As a congregation, we stand at the threshold of Heaven, seeking entry, and with our words, we beckon God to open the door, initiating a divine connection between Heaven and Earth. This initial utterance by the priest sets the overarching purpose of the forthcoming divine service: the fortification and expansion of God's Kingdom, a divine realm introduced to humanity through Jesus Christ, all for the glorification of the one true God worshipped within the Holy Trinity. The Hebrew word "Amen" concludes this statement, signifying our wholehearted agreement and acceptance.

To draw a parallel, imagine a conductor stands before an orchestra, raising the baton to signal the beginning of a symphony. In the same way, the opening declaration of the Divine Liturgy serves as our conductor's baton, reminding us that we are all part of this grand orchestration within the "concert hall" of the Nave. This signifies our journey towards the heavenly melodies of the Father, Son, and Holy Spirit—an ethereal symphony. Just as every musical composition begins with a conductor's gesture, all sacraments commence with the words, "Blessed is the kingdom of the Father and the Son and the Holy Spirit, now and forever and to the ages of ages," initiating our harmonious communion with Heaven.

A Complete Guide to The Divine Liturgy

THE DIVINE LITURGY OF SAINT JOHN CHRYSOSTOM

Priest: Blessed is the kingdom *(Mark 11:10)* of the Father and the Son and the Holy Spirit, now and forever and to the ages of ages *(cf Jude 1:25, Ephesians 3:21).*

Choir: Amen.

Notes:

_____
_____
_____
_____
_____

The Great Litany

The Orthodox Great Litany marks the initial stage of the Divine Liturgy, a moment when God eagerly awaits our prayers. It's a profound reminder that, no matter the weight of our burdens, sins, or troubles, our compassionate God stands ready to listen and provide solace.

The Great Litany, with its recurring emphasis on peace, carries a profound significance. The deacon, positioned on the ambo, symbolizes an angel guiding us in prayer, raising his stole, akin to an angel's wing, and inviting the congregation to join in prayers meticulously assembled by the Church since Apostolic times. This litany begins with an appeal for peace, recognizing that prayer cannot thrive without it. "In peace, let us pray...," "For heavenly peace...," "For peace in the whole world...," and "...for peaceful times" resound throughout. Remarkably, the term "peace" permeates the entire Divine Liturgy, a deliberate choice by the Lord and the church fathers.

This emphasis on peace is no coincidence; it addresses the myriad concerns that weigh on the minds of worshippers. The church fathers recognized the worries about family, finances, health, travel, and careers that often burden parishioners as they enter the church. Consequently, many of the prayers in the Divine Liturgy center on the quest for peace, underscoring the understanding that, in God's presence, solace and tranquility can be found amid life's challenges.

THE GREAT LITANY

Deacon: In *peace* let us pray to the Lord.

Choir: Lord, have mercy.

Priest: For the *peace* of God *(Philippians 4:7)* and the salvation of our souls, let us pray to the Lord.

Choir: Lord, have mercy.

Deacon: For *peace* in the whole world *(cf. Zechariah 1:11),* for the stability of the holy churches of God, and for the unity of all, let us pray to the Lord.

Notes:

The Orthodox Great Litany offers a profound connection with God, emphasizing the immediacy of His response to our pleas for peace. Unlike a hesitant deliberation, He grants our requests as we utter them. This divine assurance finds its roots in Matthew 18:19-20, where Christ assures us that when two or more gather in His name, the Father in Heaven will fulfill their petitions. In this sacred assembly, we affirm our awareness of God's immediate response by echoing, "**Lord, have mercy.**"

Contrary to the misconception that "**Lord, have mercy**" carries a desperate plea akin to a prisoner's plea for clemency, the Orthodox faithful understand it differently. It embodies a comforting and soothing acknowledgment of God's gracious response. It signifies a profound connection, not an arbitrary rejection. Remarkably, stepping into a church with the weight of life's burdens often leads to a sense of peace when leaving. This transformation begins with the Great Litany, sometimes referred to as "The Litany of Peace." It serves as a spiritual balm, soothing troubled hearts and minds.

Furthermore, the Great Litany beautifully reflects the Orthodox belief that God's response is immediate, as if granting peace upon our request. It reinforces the idea that, in the sacred gathering of believers, God's presence brings solace and tranquility, reaffirming the promise that where two or three are gathered in His name, He is there among them. This litany is a powerful reminder of God's continuous presence and His willingness to bring peace to the hearts of those who seek Him. A noteworthy aspect of the Great Litany is that many of its prayers are directed toward others—our President, churches, country, Archbishop, travelers—reflecting our selfless prayers for the well-being of all.

Choir: Lord, have mercy.

Deacon: For this holy temple and for those who enter it with faith, reverence, and the fear of God, let us pray to the Lord.

Choir: Lord, have mercy.

Deacon: For the Orthodox episcopate of the Russian Church; for our lord the Very Most Reverend Metropolitan _____, First Hierarch of the Russian Church Abroad; for our lord the Most Reverend _____ (*Archbishop or Bishop Name, whose diocese it is*): for the venerable priesthood, the Diaconate in Christ, for all the clergy and people, let us pray to the Lord.

Choir: Lord, have mercy.

Notes:

_____
_____
_____
_____
_____

The intriguing aspect of the Orthodox Great Litany lies in its focus on intercession for others rather than ourselves. When we encounter someone in distress—a sick friend, a grieving individual, or someone navigating a painful divorce—we often find our own problems put into perspective. It's akin to stepping out of our own thoughts and concerns. The modern term for this is "getting out of your head." When we genuinely care about and pray for others' issues, our own burdens often feel lighter.

As Christians, responding to someone's difficulties with, "I'll pray for you," is a common practice. The Great Litany within the Divine Liturgy provides a meaningful moment to fulfill that promise by offering prayers for those in need. Many Church bulletins even include lists of individuals who are suffering and in need of our prayers, often including fellow parishioners grappling with illnesses such as cancer or heart problems. Praying for these individuals during this sacred liturgical moment can profoundly impact our perspective and our hearts.

Moreover, this act of collective intercession carries significant spiritual power. While it may appear that only a few dozen or a few hundred people are praying in your local church, it's essential to recognize that there are approximately 270 million Orthodox Christians worldwide. The cumulative strength of millions of prayers ascending to God during the Great Litany, beseeching His protection for those mentioned, creates an awe-inspiring phenomenon in Heaven—an outpouring of intercession on a global scale. This collective prayer underscores the unity and compassion of the Orthodox community and exemplifies the belief in the profound impact of intercessory prayer.

Deacon: For the much suffering Russian Land and its Orthodox people both in the homeland and in the diaspora, and for their salvation, let us pray to the Lord.

Choir: Lord, have mercy.

Deacon: For this parish and city, for every city and country, and for the faithful who live in them, let us pray to the Lord.

Choir: Lord, have mercy.

Deacon: For favorable weather, an abundance of the fruits of the earth, and temperate seasons, let us pray to the Lord.

Notes:

_____
_____
_____
_____
_____

Lastly, does the Bible give us any insight in this area of the Great Litany? Yes, particularly in 1 Timothy 2:1-3. St. Paul's words, urging prayers, intercessions, and thanksgivings for all, including leaders, shed light on the profound nature of the Divine Liturgy. This litany serves as a poignant reminder that effective prayer requires inner peace and reconciliation. To approach God sincerely, one must cast aside resentment, anger, and hostility, aligning with Christ's teachings about reconciliation (Matthew 5:23-24). As the Great Litany unfolds, it extends its blessings to encompass the entire world. It highlights the interconnectedness of humanity and the Church's role in fostering harmony. Furthermore, the Litany emphasizes the power of collective prayer. The deacon, on behalf of the congregation, entrusts their lives to Christ, symbolizing unity and shared devotion. During this sacred moment, the priest intercedes for the congregation, asking the Lord to fulfill their needs. The Great Litany not only serves as a prayer but also as a profound lesson in faith, unity, and love.

Importance of Mercy & Amen

Within the Divine Liturgy, two words stand out: **"Mercy"** and **"Amen."** **"Mercy"** finds its origin in the Greek term "eleos," linked to the ancient word for soothing olive oil. In Hebrew, "eleos" signifies "steadfast love." **"Kyrie eleison,"** or **"Lord have mercy,"** essentially implores, "Lord, comfort me, relieve my pain, and grant your unwavering love." These words beckon God's compassionate response, as He showers us with His loving-kindness. In Orthodoxy, they serve as a poignant reminder of God's boundless mercy and grace.

Choir: Lord, have mercy.

Deacon: For travelers by land, sea, and air, for the sick, the suffering, the captives, and for their salvation, let us pray to the Lord.

Choir: Lord, have mercy.

Deacon: For our deliverance from all affliction, wrath, danger, and distress, let us pray to the Lord.

Choir: Lord, have mercy.

Notes:

_____
_____
_____
_____
_____

The word "Amen" is a Hebrew term with multifaceted meanings such as "certainty," "truth," and "verily." In essence, it represents our affirmative response to God. Its Hebrew root conveys a sense of firmness, confirmation, reliability, faith, and belief. Interestingly, the Bible concludes with "Amen," sealing its message: "The grace of our Lord Jesus Christ be with you all. Amen!" (Revelation 22:21). Thus, when we utter "Amen," we not only express agreement but also affirm the truth found in Scripture and the Liturgy as the bedrock of our lives. In the Russian Orthodox tradition, "Amen" is rendered as "**Аминь**" (Amin') and "Lord have Mercy" is expressed as "**Господи, помилуй**" (Gospodi, pomiluy), maintaining their original meanings and highlighting the continuity of Orthodox worship in the Greek and Hebrew languages.

Three Main Divine Liturgies

The Divine Liturgy of St. John Chrysostom: This is the most commonly celebrated liturgy among the three. St. John Chrysostom composed it, aiming to make it accessible for regular Sunday worship. It features concise prayers and hymns, making it suitable for the average churchgoer.

The Divine Liturgy of St. Basil the Great: Reserved for special events and feast days due to its theological depth and length, this liturgy was crafted by St. Basil. It incorporates extended prayers and intricate theological language, delving into the Eucharistic mystery in a profound manner.

The Divine Liturgy of the Presanctified Gifts: This liturgy is uniquely observed during Lent and Holy Week. Unlike the others, it doesn't consecrate Eucharistic elements on-site but utilizes pre-consecrated bread and wine.

Deacon: Help us, save us, have mercy upon us, and protect us, O God, by Your grace.

Choir: Lord, have mercy.

Deacon: Remembering our most holy, pure, blessed, and glorious Lady, the Theotokos and ever-virgin Mary, with all the saints, let us commit ourselves and one another and our whole life to Christ our God.

Choir: To You, O Lord.

Priest: For unto Thee are due all glory, honor, and worship: to the Father, and to the Son, and to the Holy Spirit, now and ever and unto the ages of ages.

Choir: Amen.

Notes:

Importance & Meaning of the Antiphon

In the Orthodox tradition, as the Divine Liturgy unfolds, we reach a significant point known as the Three Antiphons, which involves the chanting of hymns. Interestingly, the term "Antiphon" derives its meaning from the Greek word's "anti" and "phono," signifying "opposite" and "voice." This name signifies the practice of having two choirs, or voices, responding alternately to one another during these hymns.

The origins of this practice trace back to a vision experienced by St. Ignatius in Antioch. He envisioned angels forming two opposing choirs in Heaven, singing antiphonally, glorifying the Holy Trinity. They took turns singing, and inspired by this heavenly sight, St. Ignatius decided to separate his choir into two sections, having them sing in this antiphonal manner. Over time, this practice became the norm in Orthodox worship. During our Divine Liturgy, the Chanter recites passages from Psalm verses, while the congregation or choir acts as the "antiphon," singing in response as the passages are recited. The first antiphon or hymn is dedicated to Christ, and it also includes an invocation to the Virgin Mary, seeking her intercession on our behalf. The second antiphon similarly focuses on Christ. The third antiphon alternates, reflecting the rich liturgical tradition of Orthodox worship.

This practice of the Three Antiphons not only adds a musical dimension to the liturgy but also connects the worshipper to the heavenly choirs, offering a glimpse into the angelic worship that inspired its inception.

PRAYER OF THE FIRST ANTIPHON

Priest: Lord, our God, whose power is beyond compare, and glory is beyond understanding; whose mercy is boundless, and love for us is ineffable: Master, look upon us and upon this holy house in Your compassion. Grant to us and to those who pray with us the riches of Your mercy and compassion. For to You belongs all glory, honor, and worship to the Father and to the Son and to the Holy Spirit, now and forever and to the ages of ages.

Choir: Amen.

Notes:

Honor the Holy Theotokos, but Do Not Worship

One of the significant "misunderstandings" people often have about the Orthodox faith pertains to the veneration of the Holy Theotokos, commonly known as the Virgin Mary. Contrary to the notion of worship, Orthodox Christians hold her in the highest esteem, honoring her as the mother of Jesus, and seek her intercession in their prayers to her divine son.

The title "Theotokos" has its roots in ancient Christian writings dating back to the second and third centuries. Early Christian scholar Origen, in the third century, first used this term in surviving documents. "Theos" in Greek means God, and "tokos" signifies giving birth. When combined, they form "The one who gave birth to God."

In Orthodox theology, which reveres order and structure, the heavenly hierarchy places the Seraphim and the Cherubim closest to God. However, Orthodox believers regard the Holy Theotokos with even greater reverence, acknowledging her as "more honorable than the Cherubim, and beyond compare more glorious than the Seraphim." This demonstrates the profound esteem in which the Orthodox faith holds her.

Due to her unique closeness to her son, Jesus, Orthodox Christians beseech the Holy Theotokos to intercede on their behalf and pray for them. This practice is encapsulated in the First Antiphon, where Orthodox faithful sing, "Through the prayers of the Theotokos, Savior, save us." It signifies her role as a prayerful advocate, while recognizing that ultimate salvation comes from God Himself.

A Complete Guide to The Divine Liturgy

THE FIRST ANTIPHON

Choir: Bless the Lord, O my soul!

Blessed art Thou, O Lord!

Bless the Lord, O my soul; and all that is within me, bless His holy name!

Bless the Lord, O my soul, and forget not all His benefits. Who forgiveth all thine iniquities, Who healeth all thy dieseses.

Notes:

The Liturgy of the Catechumens & The Liturgy of the Faithful

The Divine Liturgy is divided into two parts. The first part of the Divine Liturgy, known as the Liturgy of the Word or The Liturgy of the Catechumens, serves as an instructive segment within the Orthodox worship service. Its primary focus lies in conveying the message of the Good News of Jesus Christ and the anticipation of His Kingdom. However, it is not solely an intellectual instruction; it is also a time for hymns, prayers, and the praise of God's glory.

The term "catechumen" refers to individuals in the process of converting to Christianity, receiving oral instruction before baptism. It originates from the Greek word "katechein," meaning "to instruct orally." In ancient times, catechumens and those not prepared to receive Holy Communion were required to leave the church after the sermon, symbolizing their gradual journey toward embracing the faith.

The second part of the Liturgy, known as The Liturgy of the Faithful, historically reserved for baptized Christians in good standing, has earned its name because only those firmly established in the faith could partake. This segment reaches its climax with the reception of Holy Communion, also referred to as Eucharistia, meaning "Thanksgiving." This is why it is alternatively known as the Liturgy of the Eucharist.

Interestingly, this division of the Divine Liturgy reflects the ancient practice of the early Church, emphasizing both instruction for newcomers and the profound significance of Holy Communion for the baptized faithful. This structure underscores the importance of teaching and nurturing new believers while celebrating the Eucharist as the pinnacle of worship and thanksgiving.

Choir: Who redeemeth thy life from corruption, Who crowneth thee with mercy and compassion.

Who fulfilleth thy desire with good things, thy youth is renewed like as the eagle's.

The Lord is compassionate and merciful, long-suffering and of great goodness.

Bless the Lord, O my soul, blessed art Thou, O Lord.

Notes:

First Small Litany

Between the First Antiphon and the Second Antiphon in the Divine Liturgy, there is a moment known as the "Small Litany." This brief interlude holds similarities to the Great Litany but is notably shorter in duration, hence its name. It serves as a prayerful sequence, marking a transition within the worship service.

One intriguing aspect of this liturgical practice is the consistent conclusion of litanies in the Divine Liturgy. Each litany concludes with the passage: "**Remembering our most holy, pure, blessed, and glorious Lady, the Theotokos and ever Virgin Mary, with all the saints, let us commit ourselves and one another, and our whole life to Christ our God**." This recurring formula serves as a cue, signifying the conclusion of one section of the Liturgy (in this case, the First Antiphon) and the commencement of another (in this case, the Second Antiphon). It carries a profound message, urging the congregation to remember the Virgin Mary and all the saints, while also prompting a collective commitment to surrender one's life to Christ.

This liturgical structure not only adds a sense of rhythm and flow to the Divine Liturgy but also emphasizes the significance of the Virgin Mary and the communion of saints in Orthodox worship. It encourages worshippers to unite their lives with Christ, guided by the intercession and example of these holy figures.

FIRST SMALL LITANY

Deacon: Again and again, in peace, let us pray to the Lord.
Choir: Lord, have mercy.
Deacon: Help us, save us, have mercy upon us, and protect us, O God, by Your grace.
Choir: Lord, have mercy.
Deacon: Remembering our most holy, pure, blessed, and glorious Lady, the Theotokos and ever Virgin Mary, with all the saints, let us commit ourselves and one another, and our whole life to Christ our God.
Choir: To You, O Lord.

Notes:

Meaning of Church

The term "church" commonly conjures an image of a physical place of worship. However, the Greek term "ekklesia" primarily refers to the people, not the building. Often translated as "a called-out assembly or congregation." Thus, the Church is not merely a structure but rather the gathering of those called by God. In Acts 11:26, we see "Barnabas and Saul met with the church [ekklesia]" in Antioch, highlighting the community aspect. Similarly, in 1 Corinthians 15:9, Paul acknowledges persecuting the church [ekklesia] of God. The Greek ekklesia forms the basis for "ecclesiastical" and "ecclesiology" in English, related to church matters and study.

Development of Liturgical Music

The Divine Liturgy of St. John Chrysostom has had a profound influence on the musical traditions of the Eastern Orthodox Church, most notably through its inspiration of liturgical music like the renowned "Znamenny Chant." Originating in Russia, this unique musical tradition, characterized by its distinctive melodies and notation system, is closely associated with the St. John Chrysostom Divine Liturgy. Znamenny Chant and other forms of liturgical music have evolved over time, incorporating regional variations and styles while preserving the core melodies and rhythms of the St. John Chrysostom Divine Liturgy. This rich musical heritage enhances the spiritual experience of Orthodox worshipers and adds a layer of beauty and reverence to the liturgy.

PRAYER OF THE SECOND ANTIPHON

Priest: Lord our God, save Your people and bless Your inheritance; **protect the whole body of Your Church**; sanctify those who love the beauty of Your house; glorify them in return by Your divine power; and do not forsake us who hope in You.

Priest: For Yours is the dominion, and Yours is the kingdom, the power, and the glory of the Father and the Son and the Holy Spirit, now and forever and to the ages of ages.

Choir: Amen.

Notes:

Liturgy – Psalms – Jewish Roots

The Orthodox liturgical service is deeply rooted in Jewish traditions, evident in the harmonious blend of hymns and psalms during antiphonal singing. This practice reflects a historical continuity with Jewish worship customs, where both psalms and hymns played integral roles. In Christian liturgy, the Psalms take on new significance as they intermingle with Christian hymns, creating a dynamic expression of faith.

This connection between Orthodox liturgy and its Jewish heritage is vividly demonstrated in the variable portions of the Divine Liturgy, responding to the ever-changing seasons and liturgical feasts. For instance, consider the Second Antiphon, which adapts its text to align with the specific liturgical occasion. On Sundays, the focus shifts to the resurrection of Christ, while during weekday commemorations of saints, the hymn underscores Christ's wondrous presence among His saints. Special celebrations like Christmas, Theophany, the Annunciation, Palm Sunday, the Transfiguration, the Elevation of the Cross, and Pentecost introduce distinctive hymns that resonate with the unique significance of each festal event.

This intricate interplay between the Psalms and Christian hymnody, which dynamically responds to the liturgical calendar, underscores the intrinsic link between Orthodox Christian worship and its Jewish origins. It not only enriches the liturgical experience but also serves as a powerful testament to the enduring continuity of faith and worship across centuries and diverse religious traditions.

THE SECOND ANTIPHON

Choir: Glory to the Father, and to the Son, and to the Holy Spirit. Praise the Lord, O my soul! I will praise the Lord as long as I live, I will sing praises to my God while I have being. Put not thy trust in princes, in sons of men in whom there is no salvation. When his breath departs he returns to his earth: on that very day his plans perish…

Notes:

_____
_____
_____
_____
_____

What Does the Word Liturgy Mean?

The term "Liturgy," stems from the Greek word "leitourgia." In the Greek translation of the Old Testament, it represented the sacred worship at Jerusalem's Temple. For Orthodox Christians, it has evolved into the cornerstone of communal Church worship. Termed 'the work of the people,' Liturgy, enriched by its "Divine" prefix, offers a profound connection to God's imminent Kingdom. It isn't a mere clergy performance but an active engagement of God's people who gather for worship. Interestingly, the Liturgy's transformation from a civic duty to sacred communion underscores its significance in fostering a spiritual bond among believers. It's a vivid reminder that this communal action invites active participation, not passive observation, and serves as a testament to the enduring significance of this ancient word.

Church Slavonic vs. Modern Russian

Similar to Latin in Catholicism, Church Slavonic, originating from Old Church Slavonic, was developed in the 9th century by Constantine, Methodius, and their disciples. It was based on the dialect of 9th-century Slavs in Byzantium, Greece, and remarkably understood by both Western and Eastern Slavs. Over time, uniformity eroded, and regional versions, known as 'izvods,' emerged in the 10th-11th centuries, incorporating elements from local Slavonic dialects. In the 17th century, New Church Slavonic, or the Synodal recension, emerged, synthesizing Kievan and Old Moscow versions. Though sharing some traits with Russian, it remains primarily a South Slavonic language, reserved for religious use and requiring specialized preparation for comprehension.

The Lord setteth the prisoners free, the Lord maketh wise the blind, the Lord raiseth the fallen, the Lord loveth the righteous. The Lord preserveth the sojourners, He adopteth the orphan and widow; but the way of the wicked he bringeth to ruin. The Lord will reign forever: thy God, O Zion, unto all generations.

Notes:

_____

_____

_____

_____

_____

The Hymn of Justinian

Attributed to Emperor Justinian (482-565 AD), the enclosed hymn, often called "The Hymn of Justinian," holds historical and religious significance. Justinian, renowned for constructing the Hagia Sophia, a marvel of Byzantine architecture in Constantinople, aimed to reinforce orthodox Christian beliefs through this hymn. Its lyrics resonate with The Creed's concepts, earning it the nickname "mini-Creed." This resemblance is no coincidence, as the hymn was a response to the theological controversies that roiled the early Christian Church, particularly debates about the nature of Christ. Emperor Justinian mandated the hymn's performance in churches, reflecting his dedication to consolidating Christian doctrine. Originally known as the Eisodikon, or Entrance Hymn, in Greek, it marked the Liturgy's commencement in the rite of St. James. This hymn is still an integral part of liturgical practices, emphasizing Orthodox teachings on the Son of God, Jesus Christ. The hymn eloquently describes Christ as the Only-begotten Son and Word of God, embodying both divinity and humanity. It celebrates His immortal nature, His incarnation through the Holy Theotokos and ever-Virgin Mary, and His triumph over death through His crucifixion, encapsulating the phrase "trampling down death by death." This doctrinal statement upholds the equality of the Holy Trinity: the Father, Son, and Holy Spirit. While the choir vocalizes these profound beliefs, the priest engages in a silent prayer within the altar, invoking God's blessings on the congregation and Church, and seeking divine intervention for the faithful's requests. This hymn, therefore, serves as a doctrinal pillar but also as a bridge connecting liturgical practice with the deep-rooted theological convictions of early Christianity.

Choir: Only begotten Son (*John 1:18*) and Word of God *(John 1:1)*, although immortal You humbled Yourself for our salvation, taking flesh from the holy Theotokos and ever virgin Mary and, without change, becoming man. Christ, our God, You were crucified but conquered death by death. You are one of the Holy Trinity, glorified with the Father and the Holy Spirit – save us.

THE SECOND SMALL LITANY

Deacon: Again and again, in peace, let us again pray to the Lord.

Choir: Lord, have mercy.

Deacon: Help us, save us, have mercy upon us, and protect us, O God, by Your grace.

Notes:

"Two or Three Gathered in Your Name"

The passage on the opposing page brings attention to the priest's prayer during the Divine Liturgy, where he implores God to answer the "common prayers" offered with a united heart and invokes the biblical promise that "You have promised to grant the requests of two or three gathered in Your name" (Matthew 18:19-20). This practice underscores a fundamental aspect of Orthodox Faith – the priest never celebrates the Divine Liturgy in solitude.

Beyond this, a profound revelation emerges at the conclusion of the priest's silent prayer, found on page 51. Here, he invokes God as the Creator of the unseen realm of angels, beseeching Him to dispatch these celestial beings to join the congregation's prayers and doxologies (praises). This connection signifies that the Divine Liturgy in the church is intimately intertwined with the ongoing liturgy of the angels surrounding the Throne of God. This invocation transcends mere symbolism; it is a hallmark of the uniqueness of our faith. As we worship and praise God during the Divine Liturgy, we believe that God indeed dispatches His angels, even though they remain unseen by human eyes. This profound belief underscores the reverence and decorum observed during the Divine Liturgy, for we are worshipping alongside angels who forever stand in God's presence.

This connection with the angelic realm elevates our worship experience, aligning it with the heavenly chorus that ceaselessly glorifies God. In the Orthodox tradition, this bond with the angelic host serves as a poignant reminder that our earthly liturgy mirrors the eternal worship offered in the heavenly realms.

Deacon: Remembering our most holy, pure, blessed, and glorious Lady, the Theotokos and ever Virgin Mary, with all the saints, let us commit ourselves and one another, and our whole life to Christ our God.

Choir: To You, O Lord.

PRAYER OF THE THIRD ANTIPHON

Priest (*in a low voice*): Lord, You have given us grace to offer these common prayers with one heart. You have promised to grant the requests of *two or three gathered in Your name*. Fulfill now the petitions of Your servants for our benefit, giving us the knowledge of Your truth in this world, and granting us eternal life in the world to come.

Priest: For You are a good and loving God, and to You we give glory, to the Father and the Son and the Holy Spirit, now and forever and to the ages of ages.

Choir: Amen.

Notes:

Beatitudes

The following segment, known as the third antiphon, derives its inspiration from the renowned Beatitudes delivered during the Sermon on the Mount, a pivotal teaching found in the Gospel of Matthew (Matt. 5:3-12). These Beatitudes serve as a spiritual compass, guiding Christians toward the qualities deemed essential in their faith journey.

The Beatitudes elucidate the virtues and dispositions that a devout Christian should embody. They encompass the virtues of humility, emphasizing spiritual poverty and genuine remorse for one's sins. They call for meekness when approaching the righteousness of God, emphasizing the importance of a pure heart and a compassionate spirit towards one's neighbor. Seeking peace in all circumstances, maintaining patience amidst trials, and possessing the fortitude to endure dishonor, persecution, and even death for the sake of Christ are integral aspects of this spiritual roadmap. These teachings encourage believers to trust that, as confessors of Christ and through the rigorous ascetic struggles required by such a commitment, they can anticipate a profound reward awaiting them in the heavenly realms. This concept is deeply ingrained in Christian theology, motivating individuals to persevere in their faith and strive for the virtues highlighted in the Beatitudes. Interestingly, the Beatitudes have been influential not only within Christianity but have also had a broader impact on ethical and moral philosophy, resonating with individuals seeking a deeper understanding of human virtue and righteousness. The teachings found in the Beatitudes continue to inspire and guide the lives of countless individuals seeking to align themselves with the principles of spiritual excellence and moral integrity.

THE THIRD ANTIPHON

In Thy Kingdom remember us, O Lord, when Thou comest into Thy Kingdom. Blessed are the poor in spirit, for theirs is the Kingdom of Heaven. Blessed are those who mourn, for they shall be comforted. Blessed are the meek, for they shall inherit the earth. Blessed are those who hunger and thirst after righteousness, for they shall be filled. Blessed are the merciful, for they shall obtain mercy. Blessed are the pure in heart, for they shall see God. Blessed are the peacemakers, for they shall be called the sons of God. Blessed are they that are persecuted for righteousness' sake, for theirs is the Kingdom of Heaven. Blessed are you when men shall revile you and persecute you, and say all manner of evil against you falsely for My sake. Rejoice and be exceedingly glad, for great is your reward in Heaven.

Notes:

The Small Entrance

During the Beatitudes, a pivotal moment unfolds in the Divine Liturgy known as the Small Entrance. As the Beatitudes draw to a close, the Royal Doors are opened, and the priest emerges alongside the deacon, who carries the revered Gospel through the north door onto the ambo. In a profound prayer, the priest beseeches God, the One who orchestrates the celestial armies of angels and heavenly hosts, to now enlist these celestial powers to accompany them as they make their entry into the sacred altar. This symbolic entrance with the Holy Gospel evokes the memory of Jesus Christ's initial appearance in the world when He embarked on His universal ministry. An altar boy, bearing a candle in front of the Gospel, signifies the role of John the Forerunner, who prepared the people to receive the Messiah. As the deacon stands by the Royal Doors, raising the sacred Gospel aloft and proclaiming, "**Wisdom. Let us be attentive**," an unseen reality unfolds before our eyes. Angels encompass the priest, deacon, and Gospel as they guide God's entrance into the world, a moment known as The Small Entrance. It symbolizes the divine presence entering the world and alludes to Christ's baptism. The priest's act of holding the Gospel before his face embodies the Orthodox faith's core principle: the focus is on Christ, not the priest. This profound distinction sets Orthodoxy apart from other faiths. The priest's back often turns to the congregation when at the altar, emphasizing the centrality of the Altar, where the body, blood, and Gospel of Christ are placed. This steadfast commitment to directing attention toward God, rather than any individual clergy, underscores the enduring nature of Orthodox faith over two millennia. The Orthodox faith's longevity is attributed to its unwavering focus on God.

A Complete Guide to The Divine Liturgy

THE SMALL ENTRANCE
(Entrance of the Holy Gospel)

(*The priest blesses the entrance*): Blessed is the entrance of Your saints always, now and forever and to the ages of ages. Amen.

(*He then raises the Holy Gospel Book*).

Deacon: Wisdom. Let us be attentive.

Notes:

_____
_____
_____
_____
_____

Does Orthodoxy Believe in Angels?

Absolutely! In each Liturgy, we invoke the presence of an angel to both safeguard and steer us along our paths. The scripture reminds us, "He commands His angels regarding you to guard you in all your paths ... The angel of the Lord encamps all around those who fear Him, and delivers them" (Psalm 91:11, 34:7). Etymologically, the term "angel" originates from the Greek word meaning "messenger." Angels, as spiritual beings, represent conduits through which we may discern the voice of God in our lives, provided we attentively heed the messages they bear. The teachings of St. Basil the Great underscore this notion, emphasizing that the presence of an angel remains steadfast unless repelled by our own transgressions. One captivating facet of Orthodox faith lies in its adherence to divine order. In the heavenly realm, order reigns supreme. We subscribe to the belief that God has designated a hierarchy among the angels in His divine presence. At the pinnacle of this celestial hierarchy are the Seraphim, a group of angels perpetually in God's presence, ceaselessly extolling Him with the words, "Holy, holy, holy is the Lord God Almighty, who was and is and is to come" (Book of Revelation 4:4-8).

Small Entrance Exclamation:

During the Small Entrance, Orthodox faithful stand upright, symbolizing attentiveness. "Orthi," Greek for correct posture, underscores focus. They view the Holy Gospel as Christ Himself, ready for His teachings. "O come, let us worship..." invites reverence. "Alleluia" in Hebrew means "Praise the Lord," enriching worship exaltation.

Choir: Come, let us worship and bow before Christ. Save us, O Son of God (*who rose from the dead*), to You we sing: Alleluia.

(*The priest enters the sanctuary. The Apolytikion is repeated and the Troparion of the church and the Kontakion of the day are sung.*)

THE TRISAGION HYMN

Deacon: Let us pray to the Lord.

Choir: Lord, have mercy.

Notes:

_____
_____
_____
_____
_____

The Trisagion Hymn

The term Trisagion derives from the Greek words "Tria" (meaning "Three") and "Agios" (meaning "Holy"), hence, in this hymn, "Holy" is repeated three times.

The Trisagion Hymn exemplifies how Orthodox faithful on earth worship God just as He is worshiped in Heaven. This celestial worship is depicted in the Bible, where the Prophet Isaiah recounts his vision: "I saw the Lord sitting on a throne… Above Him were seraphs… And one called to another and said: 'Holy, holy, holy is the Lord of hosts; the whole earth is full of His glory!'" (Isaiah 6:1-5).

Similarly, in the Book of Revelation, John describes his heavenly vision: "Each of the four living creatures had six wings and was covered with eyes all around, even under his wings. Day and night they never stop saying: 'Holy, Holy, Holy is the Lord God Almighty, who was, and is, and is to come.'" (Revelation 4:8).

Why is "Holy" repeated three times in both visions? This repetition underscores the holiness of the Trinity: God the Father, God the Son, and God the Holy Spirit. This trifold declaration highlights the distinct yet unified nature of the Holy Trinity, a core belief in Orthodox Christianity.

The Trisagion Hymn, therefore, is not merely a song but a profound reflection of heavenly worship, bringing a piece of divine liturgy to earth, reinforcing the faithful's connection to the divine.

Priest (*in a low voice*): Holy God, You dwell among Your saints. You are praised by the Seraphim with the thrice holy hymn *(Isaiah 6:2-3)* and glorified by the Cherubim and worshipped by all the heavenly powers. You have brought all things out of nothing into being *(cf 2 Macc 7:28)*. You have created man and woman in Your image and likeness *(Genesis 1:27)* and adorned them with all the gifts of Your grace. You give wisdom and understanding *(2 Chronicles 1:10)* to the supplicant and do not overlook the sinner but have established repentance as the way of salvation. You have enabled us, Your lowly and unworthy servants, to stand at this hour before the glory of Your holy altar and to offer to You due worship and praise.

Notes:

_____
_____
_____
_____
_____

Notice how Revelation mentions, "...and the house was filled with smoke." This imagery reflects the Orthodox tradition of filling the church with incense, mirroring heavenly worship.

The Trisagion Hymn has its roots in the visions of Isaiah and John. Isaiah's ecstasy revealed the Seraphim crying, "Holy, Holy, Holy is the Lord of Hosts" (Isaiah 6:3). Similarly, John's vision depicted heavenly worshipers proclaiming, "Holy, holy, holy, Lord God Almighty, Who was, and is, and is to come!" (Revelation 4:8).

By singing this hymn, the Church elevates the hearts of the faithful, inviting them to contemplate the Lord's glory and join the heavenly hosts in worship. This practice symbolizes the unity of earthly and heavenly worship, drawing believers closer to the divine presence. Through the Trisagion, the faithful participate in a timeless act of praise, connecting with the eternal worship of God in Heaven.

Master, accept the thrice-holy hymn also from the lips of us sinners and visit us in Your goodness. Forgive our voluntary and involuntary transgressions, sanctify our souls and bodies, and grant that we may worship and serve You in holiness all the days of our lives, by the intercessions of the holy Theotokos and of all the saints who have pleased You throughout the ages.

Priest: For You are holy, our God, and to You we give glory, to the Father and the Son and the Holy Spirit, now and forever . . .

Deacon: And to the ages of ages.

Choir: Amen. *Holy God, Holy Mighty, Holy Immortal, have mercy on us (3x).*

Who Decides the Epistle Readings?

The Church follows a lectionary, an established order of readings from the seventh century. Throughout the year, it systematically reads the writings of the Apostles in the sequence they appear in the New Testament.

ARE WE AN EVANGELICAL CHURCH?

Absolutely! The term "evangelical" comes from the Greek word "evangelistes," meaning "one who delivers the good news." The life, ministry, death, and resurrection of Jesus Christ are the ultimate Good News. The Gospel of Christ primarily announces what God has accomplished through Jesus.

The word "evangelistes" dates back to 490 BC, following the Battle of Marathon. After the outnumbered Athenians triumphed over the Persians, a messenger named Pheidippides ran 25 miles to Athens to deliver the victorious news. Upon arrival, he proclaimed, "Hairete! Nenikamen!" – "Rejoice! We have conquered!"

This declaration mirrors the Gospel of Christ: "Rejoice! We've won!" The message underscores the victory and hope offered through Jesus Christ, affirming the essence of being an evangelical church.

THE EPISTLE

The term "Epistle" originates from the Greek word meaning "to send news," and is synonymous with "letter." The New Testament epistles, primarily authored by the Apostle Paul, were directed to various communities and intended for public reading. These letters aimed to help early Christian communities understand Christ and deepen their faith. Remarkably, nearly two thousand years later, these epistles continue to be read in congregations, guiding modern believers in their spiritual growth.

St. John Chrysostom eloquently emphasizes the importance of hearing and learning from the epistles: "Listen, those of you living in the world who have a wife and children, how St. Paul commends particularly to you the reading of scripture... For as the rich, with money, can bear fines and damages, so he that is rich in the doctrines of philosophy [Scripture] will be able to bear not only poverty but all calamities... get yourself at least the New Testament, the Apostolic Epistles, the Acts, the Gospels, for your constant teachers. If grief befalls you, dive into them as into a chest of medicines; take comfort from your trouble, be it loss, or death, or bereavement of relations; or rather dive not into them merely, but take them wholly into yourself; keep them in your mind. For not knowing the scripture is the cause of all evils. In doing so, we go into battle without arms, and then how are we to come off safe?"

During the reading of the Epistle, the priest performs a censing, symbolizing the Grace of the Holy Spirit by which the Apostles spread Jesus Christ's teachings to the world. Congregants should respond to both the censing and the priest's exclamation, "Peace be unto all," with a simple bow, without making the sign of the Cross. This act signifies reverence and readiness to receive the divine message.

(The priest, turning toward the prothesis, says in a low voice:)
Blessed is He who comes in the name of the Lord *(Psalm 118:26)*. Blessed are You, seated on the throne of glory in Your kingdom, seated upon the Cherubim *(Daniel 3:54-55; Psalm 98:1)* always, now and forever and to the ages of ages. Amen.

THE EPISTLE

(Apostolic reading)

Deacon: Let us attend.

Priest: Peace be unto all.

Reader: And unto thy spirit.

Deacon: Wisdom.

Reader: The prokeimenon ...

Choir: *repeats the prokeimenon ...*

Deacon: Wisdom.

Reader: The reading of the Holy Epistle of Saint Paul the Apostles to _____.

Deacon: Let us attend.

Reader: *reads the epistle.*

Notes:

_____

_____

_____

_____

_____

THE HOLY GOSPEL

During every Liturgy, readings are taken from one of the four Gospels—Matthew, Mark, Luke, and John. These texts recount the life, teachings, crucifixion, and resurrection of Jesus. The term "Gospel" comes from the Old English "God-spel," meaning "glad tidings" or "Good News."

1. **The Gospel of Mark** is believed by modern scholars to be the earliest written, around AD 65-70. It served as a source for both Luke and Matthew. Tradition holds that Mark was a companion of Peter, who shared the Good News with him.

2. **The Gospel of Luke** aims to "write an orderly account" of Jesus' life and was composed between AD 80-90. Luke is thought to be a second-generation Christian, familiar with eyewitnesses. Traditionally regarded as a physician and follower of Paul, Luke not only provides a Gospel but also the Book of Acts, detailing the early Church's history.

3. **The Gospel of Matthew**, written between AD 60-85, is traditionally attributed to the apostle Matthew, a former tax collector. Some early Church Fathers believed it was originally penned in Aramaic, Jesus' language, though most scholars agree our version was written in Greek. Due to their similarities, Matthew, Mark, and Luke are referred to as the Synoptic Gospels, derived from the Greek "syn-" (together) and "opsis" (seeing).

Priest: Peace be unto you.

Reader: And unto thy spirit.

Deacon: Wisdom.

Reader: Alleluia.

Choir: Alleluia....

PRAYER OF THE GOSPEL

Priest *(in a low voice)*: Illumine our hearts with the incorruptible light of Thy knowledge, O Master, Lover of mankind, and open the eyes of our mind to the understanding of Thy Gospel teachings. Implant in us also the fear of Thy blessed commandments, that, trampling down all lusts of the flesh, we may pursue a spiritual way of life, being mindful of and doing all that is well-pleasing unto Thee. For Thou art the illumination of our souls and bodies, O Christ our God, and unto Thee do we send up glory, together with Thine unoriginate Father, and Thine all-holy, good, and life-giving Spirit, now and ever and unto the ages of ages. Amen.

Notes:

_____

_____

_____

_____

_____

4. **The Gospel of John**, written between AD 80-95, stands out for its distinct style and deep theological focus. Tradition suggests that St. John, aware of the other Gospels, intentionally composed a unique narrative. Although we now have all four Gospels in a single volume, each originated from different early Christian communities.

These four Gospels gradually gained recognition as the most authoritative accounts of Christ's life and teachings. While numerous other gospels and writings about Jesus existed, they were not deemed suitable for public reading. The four Gospels we have today are considered the oldest and most reliable sources about Christ.

Moreover, the term "Gospel" often refers to the message itself, not just a collection of books. It represents the most crucial message in history. During the Liturgy, when the Priest reads the Gospel from the Royal Doors, the congregation stands to signify Christ's presence and His words being spoken to us.

The candle held by the altar boy during this time symbolizes the all-illuminating Light of Christ, guiding us in faith and life toward the Kingdom of eternal light. Traditionally, a sermon follows the Gospel reading to expound on the meanings of the Epistle and Gospel passages. In some services, this sermon may be delivered at the end.

This tradition of standing for the Gospel reading and the illuminating candle underscores the profound reverence and importance of Christ's teachings, highlighting the continuity and depth of the Orthodox faith. The integration of these practices connects the faithful with the divine light and wisdom conveyed through the Scriptures, enriching the spiritual experience.

THE HOLY GOSPEL

Deacon: Bless, Master, him who proclaims the good tidings of the holy Apostle and Evangelist _____.

Priest: May God, through the prayers of the holy, glorious, and all laudable Apostle and Evangelist _____, enable you to proclaim the glad tidings with great power, to the fulfillment of the gospel of His beloved Son, our Lord Jesus Christ.

Deacon: Amen.

Deacon: Wisdom! Let us attend! Let us listen to the Holy Gospel.

Priest: Peace be unto all.

Choir: And to your spirit.

Deacon: The reading from the Holy Gospel according to St. _____.

Deacon: Let us attend.

Deacon / Priest: *reads the Gospel.*

Priest: Peace be unto you who have proclaimed the Gospel.

Choir: Glory to Thee, O Lord, glory to Thee.

Notes:

_____
_____
_____
_____
_____

Litany of Fervent Supplication

After the Gospel, the Litany of Fervent Supplication is recited, inviting the faithful to pray to the Lord with pure hearts and all their soul's strength. This litany resembles the Great Litany but emphasizes fervor with the repeated plea, "Lord, have mercy."

In this prayer, we seek the Lord's compassion for life, peace, health, salvation, and forgiveness of the sins of the parishioners, referred to as the "brethren of this holy and all-venerable temple." The final petition acknowledges those who actively contribute to the parish—those who minister, chant, read, and serve, as well as the congregation awaiting God's abundant mercy.

The litany also highlights those who bring offerings and do good works for the church. These contributions include providing essentials for the divine service, such as oil, incense, and prosphoras, as well as monetary and material gifts for the church's beauty and upkeep. Additionally, it recognizes those who support poor parishioners and address other religious and moral needs within the community.

This tradition of fervent supplication reinforces the communal and compassionate nature of the Orthodox faith, where the prayers and contributions of each member help sustain and enrich the spiritual life of the entire parish. The repetition of "Lord, have mercy" reflects the earnest and heartfelt nature of these prayers, drawing the faithful closer to God's grace and mercy.

LITANY OF FERVENT SUPPLICATION

Deacon: Let us all say with all our soul and with all our mind, let us say.

Choir: Lord, have mercy.

Deacon: O Lord almighty, the God of our fathers, we pray to Thee, hearken and have mercy.

Deacon: Have mercy on us, O God, according to Thy great mercy, we pray to Thee, hearken and have mercy.

Choir: Lord, have mercy (*3x*).

Deacon: Again, we pray for the Orthodox episcopate of the Russian Church Abroad, for the Most Reverend Metropolitan _____, First Hierarch of Russian Church Abroad; for the Most Reverend Archbishop _____ for the Most Reverend Bishop _____; and all our brethren in Christ.

Deacon: Again, we pray for the suffering Russian Land and its people both in the homeland and in the Diaspora in grievous circumstances, and for their salvation, for this land and its authorities.

Deacon: Again, we pray for our brethren, the presbyters, the hieromonks, and for all our brethren in Christ.

Deacon: Again, we pray for the blessed and ever-memorable holy Orthodox patriarchs, and for the blessed and evermemorable founders of this holy temple, and for all our fathers and brethren gone to their rest before us, and the Orthodox here and everywhere laid to rest.

Deacon: Again, we pray for those who bring offerings and do good works in this holy and all venerable temple, for those who minister and those who chant, and for all the people present who await Thy great and abundant mercy.

Priest: For Thou art a merciful God, and the Lover of mankind, and unto thee do we send up glory: to the Father, and to the Son, and to the Holy Spirit ...

Choir: Amen.

Notes:

Litany for the Catechumens

Next, the Litany for the Catechumens is chanted. This prayer asks the Lord to have mercy on those preparing to join the Church and to establish them in the true faith. During this litany, the priest unfolds the antimins on the Holy Table, the catechumens are asked to leave the church, and the Liturgy of the Faithful begins.

Although the institution of catechumens is no longer in regular practice, the litany remains to remind the faithful of the vows made at Baptism and the apostolic duty to help others join the true Church.

The antimins, meaning "in place of the table," is a special cloth depicting the burial of Christ. It is blessed and signed by the bishop for the celebration of the Liturgy. This tradition dates back to times of persecution when the Church had no permanent place of worship and could not transport the Holy Table. Instead, the antimins was taken to where the Liturgy was to be celebrated. The Liturgy cannot proceed without the antimins, so its preservation is the priest's responsibility if anything happens to the church.

This practice highlights the importance of the antimins as a symbol of continuity and resilience in the face of adversity. It serves as a reminder of the Church's perseverance through persecution and its commitment to maintaining the sanctity of the Liturgy, regardless of circumstances. The presence of the antimins ensures that the faithful can continue to celebrate the Liturgy, keeping alive the memory of Christ's sacrifice and the early Church's struggles.

LITANY OF THE CATECHUMENS

Deacon: Pray, ye catechumens, unto the Lord.

Choir: Lord, have mercy.

Deacon: Ye faithful, let us pray for the catechumens, that the Lord will have mercy on them.

Deacon: That He will catethize them with the word of truth.

Deacon: That He will reveal unto them the gospel of righteousness.

Deacon: That He will unite them to His Holy, Catholic, and Apostolic Church.

Deacon: Save them, have mercy on them, help them, and keep them, O God, by Thy grace.

Deacon: Ye catechumens, bow your heads unto the Lord.

Choir: To Thee, Lord.

Priest: That with us they may glorify Thine all honorable and majestic name: of the Father, and of the Son, and of the Holy Spirit, now and ever and unto the ages of ages.

Choir: Amen.

Notes:

The Liturgy of the Faithful

The third part of the Liturgy is known as the Liturgy of the Faithful. This segment is reserved for those already baptized, and it can be divided into several key sections:

1. the transferring of the honorable Gifts from the Table of Preparation to the Holy Table,
2. the preparation of the faithful for the sacrifice of the Gifts,
3. the sacrifice (changing) of the Gifts,
4. the preparation of the faithful for Communion,
5. Communion,
6. and the thanksgiving after Communion and the Dismissal.

After the catechumens are asked to depart, two short litanies are proclaimed. During these litanies, the priest offers a heartfelt prayer:

"Again and oftimes we fall down before Thee and pray unto Thee, O Good One and Lover of mankind, that looking down upon our supplication Thou wouldst cleanse our souls and bodies from all defilement of flesh and spirit; and grant us to stand blameless and uncondemned before Thy holy altar. Grant also to those who pray with us, O God, growth in life and faith and spiritual understanding. Grant them always to worship Thee blamelessly with fear and love, and to partake without condemnation of Thy Holy Mysteries and grant that they may be accounted worthy of Thy Heavenly Kingdom."

This part of the Liturgy underscores the deep spiritual preparation and reverence required for the faithful to partake in the Holy Mysteries.

THE LITURGY OF THE FAITHFUL

Deacon: All catechumens, depart. Depart, catechumens. All that are catechumens, depart. Let no catechumen remain. Let us, the faithful, again and again in peace, pray unto the Lord. Choir: Lord, have mercy.

Deacon: Help us, save us, have mercy on us, and keep us, O God, by Thy grace.

Deacon: Wisdom!

Priest: For unto Thee are due all glory, honor, and worship: to the Father, and to the Son, and to the Holy Spirit, now and ever and unto ages of ages.

Choir: Amen.

Deacon: Again and again in peace let us pray unto the Lord. Choir: Lord, have mercy.

Deacon: Help us, save us, have mercy on us, and keep us, O God, by Thy grace.

Deacon: Wisdom!

Priest: That guarded always by Thy might we may send up glory unto Thee: to the Father, and to the Son, and to the Holy Spirit, now and ever and unto the ages of ages.

Choir: Amen.

It highlights the importance of approaching the altar with a pure heart and the profound sense of community as the faithful pray together for spiritual growth and understanding. The Liturgy of the Faithful serves as a powerful reminder of the sacredness of Communion and the collective journey towards the Heavenly Kingdom.

Cherubic Hymn

The Cherubic Hymn follows, marking a significant moment when the faithful are invited to set aside daily concerns and present themselves in a manner akin to the Cherubim, who are closest to God in Heaven. This hymn, which praises God with the thrice-holy exclamation, is sung while the deacon performs a censing. Meanwhile, the priest prays privately for the purification of his soul and heart, seeking the Holy Spirit's strength to offer the Gifts with reverence. The Cherubic Hymn is recited quietly three times by the priest and deacon before they process to transfer the Gifts from the Table of Preparation to the Holy Table. This solemn procession is known as the **Great Entry**, symbolizing the faithful's transition from earthly concerns to divine worship.

> **The Great Entrance**
>
> The Great Entrance involves carrying the bread and wine (the gifts) from the Chapel of the Prothesis, located on the north side of the sanctuary, to the Altar. At this stage, they remain as bread and wine, not yet the body and blood of Christ. This procession mirrors Christ's triumphant entry into Jerusalem on Palm Sunday, symbolizing His arrival and preparation for the ultimate sacrifice.

CHERUBIC HYMN

Choir: Let us who mystically represent the Cherubim and chant the thrice-holy hymn unto the life-giving Trinity, now lay aside all earthly cares.

(While the Cherubic Hymn is being sung, the Priest prays in a low voice:) No one bound by worldly desires and pleasures *(Tit 3:3, cf. 1 Pet 2:11)* is worthy to approach, draw near or minister to You, the King of glory *(Psalm 24:78)*. To serve You is great and awesome even for the heavenly powers. On account of Your ineffable and immeasurable love for us, You became man without alteration or change. You have served as our High Priest, *(cf. Heb 5:4-6)* and as Lord of All *(Job 5:8)*, have entrusted to use the celebration of this liturgical sacrifice without the shedding of blood. For You alone, Lord our God, rule over all things in Heaven and on earth. *(1 Chron. 29:11)* You are seated on the throne of the Cherubim *(Psalm 98:1)*, the Lord of the Seraphim and the king of Israel *(Zp 3:15; John 1:49)*. You alone are holy and dwell among your saints

(Is 57:15; Ps 24:6). You alone are good and ready to hear. Therefore, I implore you, look upon me, Your sinful and unworthy servant *(Mt 25:30; Lk17:10),* and cleanse my soul and heart from evil consciousness *(cf Heb 10:22).*

Notes:

A Special Moment

After the priest has prepared the gifts, we have sung hymns, and heard the word of God, the highlighted passage instructs us to "set aside all the cares of life" to receive God fully. This sentiment is palpable during the Great Entrance, where a sense of quiet reverence prevails.

The Great Entrance reflects an ancient practice: early Christians would bring their offerings of bread and wine to the Narthex, where deacons would carry them to the altar for consecration. Today, the prosphora, meaning "offering," is typically baked by parishioners and brought to the church in advance, while wine for Communion is often donated by others.

The solemnity of the procession signifies that "the King of all" is accompanied invisibly by angelic orders, echoing the original Greek term for "upborne," which translates to "borne aloft as on spears." This term harks back to an ancient custom where a nation's leader, seated on shields held aloft on spears, was paraded through the streets to demonstrate their exaltation. This imagery underscores the reverence with which we approach the Divine during the Liturgy.

Enable me by the power of Your Holy Spirit (*Luke 4:14, Rom 15:13*) so that, vested with the grace of the priesthood, I may stand before Your holy Table and celebrate the mystery of Your holy and pure Body and Your precious Blood. To you I come with bowed head and pray: do not turn Your face away from me (*Psalm 143:7*) nor reject me from among Your children (*Wis 9:4*), but make me, Your sinful and unworthy servant, worthy to offer to You these gifts. For You, Christ our God, are the Offerer and the Offered, the One who receives and is distributed, and to You we give glory, together with Your eternal Father and Your holy, good, and life-giving Spirit, now and forever and to the **ages of ages**. Amen.

*(The Priest censes and recites in a low voice the "Cherubic Hymn," "Having Beheld Christ's **Resurrection**" (on Sundays), and the 50th Psalm. Then the Great Entrance takes place.)*

(The priest enters the sanctuary, while the people sing the end of the Cherubic Hymn.)

Notes:

_____
_____
_____
_____
_____

What Vestments Does the Clergy Wear?
Some Clergy Vestments:

1. **Epitrachelion (Stole)**: A long, narrow vestment worn around the neck by priests and bishops, symbolizing the grace of the Holy Spirit.
2. **Phelonion**: A large, cape-like vestment worn by priests, representing the righteousness of Christ.
3. **Sakkos**: A vestment similar to the phelonion, worn by bishops instead of the phelonion.
4. **Sticharion**: A long-sleeved garment worn by all clergy, symbolizing the baptismal garment of purity.
5. **Zone (Belt)**: A belt worn by the priest or bishop over the sticharion, symbolizing strength for service.
6. **Epigonation (Palitsa)**: A diamond-shaped vestment worn on the right side by some clergy, representing spiritual warfare.
7. **Omophorion**: A wide band of cloth worn by bishops over the shoulders, symbolizing the lost sheep being carried by Christ.
8. **Mitre**: A crown-like headpiece worn by bishops, representing their authority and the crown of thorns.
9. **Orarion**: A narrow band of cloth worn by deacons over one shoulder, symbolizing the wings of angels.

The Great Entrance

During the Great Entrance, the faithful stand with bowed heads, praying that the Lord will remember them and their loved ones in His Kingdom. After the priest's blessing, "and all of you Orthodox Christians, may the Lord God remember in His Kingdom," the congregation responds softly, "And may the Lord God remember thy priesthood in His Kingdom, always, now and ever and unto the ages of ages."

This solemn procession symbolizes Christ's journey to His voluntary suffering and crucifixion. The priest places the chalice and bread—representing the Body of Christ—on the Holy Table, mirroring the placement of Christ's body in the tomb. The Royal Doors are closed, symbolizing the entrance to Christ's tomb, and the curtain is drawn as if guarding the Sepulcher.

In this moment, the priest recites a poignant prayer: "The noble Joseph, having taken down Thine immaculate Body from the tree, wrapped It in pure linen and anointed It with spices, and laid It in a new tomb. In the tomb with the body and in hell with the soul, in paradise with the thief and on the throne with the Father and the Spirit, wast Thou, Who fillest all things, O uncircumscribed Christ. More life-giving and more beautiful than paradise, and truly more radiant than any royal chamber is Thy tomb, O Christ, the fountain of our resurrection."

This ritual reflects an ancient tradition of commemorating Christ's burial and resurrection, and underscores the continuity of Orthodox worship with the early Christian practices.

THE GREAT ENTRANCE

Deacon: The Orthodox episcopate of the Russian Church Abroad, the Most Reverend Metropolitan _____, First Hierarch of Russian Church Abroad; the Most Reverend Archbishop_____ the Most Reverend Bishop_____; the priesthood and the monastics may the Lord remember them in His kingdom, now and ever and unto ages of ages.

Deacon: The suffering Russian Land and its people both in the homeland and in the Diaspora in grievous circumstances, may the Lord remember them in His kingdom now and ever and unto ages of ages.

Deacon: The President of this country, all civil authorities, and the armed forces may the Lord remember them in His kingdom, now and ever and unto ages of ages.

Deacon: The founders of this holy temple, all parishioners, the chanters and all Orthodox Christians may the Lord God remember in His Kingdom, always now and ever and unto the ages of ages.

Choir: Amen. That we may receive the King of all who cometh invisibly upborne by the angelic hosts. Alleluia! Alleluia! Alleluia!

Notes:

_____
_____
_____
_____

Importance of the Sign of the Cross

The Sign of the Cross is a profound and ancient Christian practice symbolizing blessing and devotion to Christ. Tertullian (c. 160-240), an early Christian writer from North Africa, noted its significance: "We Christians wear out our foreheads with the Sign of the Cross." This gesture integrates the entire body into a declaration of faith.

Over centuries, the Sign of the Cross has evolved in its form and significance. The Eastern Orthodox tradition, which has been standardized since the seventeenth century, involves a distinctive method: the thumb, index, and middle fingers are held together, while the ring and pinky fingers rest against the palm. This hand position symbolizes the unity of the Holy Trinity—Father, Son, and Holy Spirit—with the three fingers representing the three Persons of the Godhead and the two pressed fingers denoting Christ's dual nature as both fully human and fully divine.

The motion of the cross—touching the forehead, chest, right shoulder, and left shoulder—mirrors the structure of the cross itself. As this gesture is made, the worshiper recites, "In the name of the Father" at the forehead, "and of the Son" at the navel, and "and of the Holy Spirit, Amen" as they cross the shoulders. This practice symbolizes an offering of one's whole self to God: mind (forehead), soul (navel), strength (right shoulder), and heart (left shoulder).

Traditionally, the Sign of the Cross is performed before veneration of icons, during the reading of the Gospel, while lighting candles, and whenever the Holy Trinity or the Virgin Mary is mentioned, signifying reverence and the embrace of divine grace.

Lots of Candles

Candles are a striking feature in Orthodox churches, appearing in various contexts from the narthex to baptismal services, marriages, and even Easter celebrations. Their prominence is deeply rooted in history. In ancient Rome, candles were used in ceremonies to honor high dignitaries, symbolizing their importance and divine favor. This practice influenced Christian rituals, where candles now symbolize the divine light of Christ.

In Orthodox worship, candles serve multiple symbolic purposes. During the Little Entrance, candles are carried to highlight the significance of the Gospel of Christ, representing its divine authority and illumination. The use of candles as a symbol of joy is tied to the belief that Christ is "the light of the World," dispelling spiritual darkness and guiding the faithful.

Candles also reflect the light of Christ's teachings and presence, enhancing the reverent atmosphere of Orthodox services. They are lit before icons, during readings, and in various rituals, embodying the ongoing divine presence and the illumination of the Church's spiritual life.

Remembering Death

The Orthodox Liturgy reminds us of our mortality, a reality we often prefer to avoid. For Orthodox Christians, however, death is viewed not as an end but as an encounter with the Risen Christ and a gateway to "eternal life" (John 3:16). As St. Paul assures us, "to die is gain" (Philippians 1:22), and we are called to "not grieve as others do who have no hope" (1 Thessalonians 4:13). "Here we have no lasting city but are looking for the city that is to come" (Hebrews 13:14).

Monastic writers emphasize the "remembrance of death" as a guiding principle for living. Metropolitan Anthony Bloom (1914-2003) reflected on this: "Death is the touchstone of our attitude to life. People who are afraid of death are afraid of life. It is impossible not to be afraid of life with all its complexity and dangers if one is afraid of death. This means that to solve the problem of death is not a luxury. If we are afraid of death we will never be prepared to take ultimate risks; we will spend our life in a cowardly, careful, and timid manner. It is only if we can face death, make sense of it, and determine its place and our place in regard to it that we will be able to live in a fearless way and to the fullness of our ability. Too often we wait until the end of our life to face death, whereas we would have lived quite differently if only we had faced death at the outset."

Who are the Typical Participants in the Liturgy?

In the Orthodox Divine Liturgy, several key participants serve specific roles:

1. **Bishop** (if present): Oversees the Liturgy, symbolizing Church unity and consecrating the Eucharist.
2. **Priest**: Leads the service, offers the bread and wine, and administers Holy Communion.
3. **Deacon**: Assists the priest, leads litanies, reads the Gospel, and helps with Communion.
4. **Subdeacon** (if present): Assists in preparing the altar and sacred vessels.
5. **Reader**: Reads the Epistle and other scriptures, chants Psalms.
6. **Acolytes** (Altar Servers): Assist with candles, the censer, and other tasks around the altar.
7. **Choir**: Leads the congregation in singing hymns and responses.
8. **Congregation**: Participates in singing, responding to prayers, and receiving Communion.

Each role contributes to the communal worship experience, emphasizing the hierarchical and participatory nature of the service.

Litany of Supplication

The petitions during this part of the Liturgy may initially seem similar to the Great Litany from earlier, but they actually reflect a shift in focus. While the Great Litany primarily interceded for others—such as the Archbishop, priests, our nation, travelers, and the suffering—these petitions center more on our personal needs and spiritual well-being.

Instead of asking for material blessings, these prayers address profound human needs. They seek deliverance from affliction, protection from wrath and danger, and a life marked by peace and holiness. Requests include: "For our deliverance from affliction," "Help us, have mercy upon us, and protect us," "For an angel of peace, a faithful guardian of our souls," and "For a Christian end to our lives, peaceful and without shame."

These supplications emphasize spiritual and personal dimensions of life. They request a peaceful, sinless day and a serene conclusion to our earthly journey, preparing us for a favorable judgment before Christ. The invocation for an "angel of peace" underscores the beauty and depth of these prayers.

This moment provides a profound opportunity for personal reflection and preparation. It helps align our hearts and minds for Communion, inviting us to seek divine aid in our personal lives and to approach the sacrament with a purified spirit.

(After placing the holy gifts on the holy Table, the priest says:)

LITANY OF SUPPLICATION

Deacon: Let us complete our prayer to the Lord.

Choir: Lord, have mercy.

Deacon: For the precious gifts here presented, let us pray to the Lord.

Choir: Lord, have mercy.

Notes:

_____
_____
_____
_____
_____

Praying the Bible in the Liturgy

Orthodox Christians engage with the Bible not just through reading but through praying it, a practice vividly embodied in the Liturgy of St. John Chrysostom. Each Sunday, the Liturgy includes readings from the New Testament—a selection from the Epistles and the Gospel. Beyond these readings, the Liturgy integrates prayers and hymns that echo the Bible's language and themes.

For example, the Lord's Prayer and selections from the Book of Psalms are integral to the service. The priest's blessing, "The grace of our Lord Jesus Christ and the love of God the Father and the communion of the Holy Spirit be with you all," echoes St. Paul's farewell in 2 Corinthians 13:13. Similarly, the hymn "Holy, Holy, Holy Lord God of Sabaoth, Heaven and Earth are full of Your glory" reflects the song of the Cherubim from Isaiah 6:1-5.

The Liturgy's prayers are richly infused with biblical imagery and quotations. Paul Evdokimov, a renowned French Orthodox theologian, noted that the prayers of the Liturgy contain 98 references to the Old Testament and 114 to the New Testament. Thus, the Liturgy is not merely a service; it is a living expression of Scripture, where the language and themes of the Bible are woven throughout every part of the worship experience.

Deacon: For this holy temple and for those who enter it with faith, reverence, and the fear of God, *let us pray to the Lord.*

Choir: Lord, have mercy.

Deacon: For our deliverance from all affliction, wrath, danger, and distress, *let us pray to the Lord.* **People**: Lord, have mercy.

Deacon: Help us, save us, have mercy upon us, and protect us, O God, by Your grace.

Choir: Lord, have mercy.

Notes:
_____
_____
_____
_____
_____

Attending the Liturgy attentively teaches us to pray the Bible. The Church's worship elements—priesthood, vestments, altar, tabernacle, oil lamps, and incense—are drawn from Old Testament practices in Exodus, Leviticus, and Psalms. These elements symbolize the Christological fulfillment of ancient Israel's worship as described in the New Testament's Letter to the Hebrews. The Divine Liturgy celebrates how Christ's death and resurrection fulfill every aspect of the Old Testament Passover and Exodus, transforming these ancient rituals into a new covenant of grace and salvation.

Guard the doors. **Wisdom. Let us be attentive.**

Before reciting the Creed, the deacon or priest would ensure the church doors were closed and guarded. This practice dates back to early Christianity when confessing faith could be dangerous and even life-threatening. The safeguarding of the congregation allowed them to boldly proclaim their Christian beliefs with the assurance of safety during these perilous times.

Deacon: For a perfect, holy, peaceful, and sinless day, let us ask the Lord.

Choir: Grant this, O Lord.

Deacon: For an angel of peace, a faithful guide, a guardian of our souls and bodies, let us ask the Lord.

People: Grant this, O Lord.

Deacon: For forgiveness and remission of our sins and transgressions, let us ask the Lord.

Choir: Grant this, O Lord.

Notes:

_____
_____
_____
_____
_____

Remembering the Saints

In the Liturgy, we are prompted to "remember all the saints." But who are these saints? Saints are individuals who have lived out their faith in Jesus Christ with exceptional devotion, often enduring great trials or martyrdom for their beliefs. They are celebrated figures from every era and culture who have been officially recognized by the Church for their exemplary Christian life.

Saints like Peter, John, and the apostles, as well as martyrs such as Barbara, and other saints John Chrysostom, Seraphim of and John of Shanghai & San Francisco, have been canonized not because they were made saints by the Church, but because their sanctity was evident in their lives. Canonization is a formal recognition of their holiness and a confirmation that their lives were exemplary models of Christian virtue.

The term "canonization" comes from the Greek word "kanon," meaning "rule" or "standard," and refers to the inclusion of a saint's name in the official list of saints, or canon. This canon is read during various liturgical services, including Orthros or Matins. Each day of the year honors a number of saints, reminding the faithful of these models of piety and virtue.

Deacon: For all that is good and beneficial to our souls, and for peace in the world, let us ask the Lord.

Choir: Grant this, O Lord.

Deacon: For the completion of our lives in peace and repentance, let us ask the Lord.

Choir: Grant this, O Lord.

Notes:
_____
_____
_____
_____
_____

When a Christian's name is included in the canon of saints, it signifies that the Church encourages the faithful to seek that saint's intercession before God. Special liturgical services may be composed in the saint's honor and celebrated by the Church. For the first thousand years of Church history, saints were recognized without any formal canonization process. Local congregations would remember notable Christians during their liturgical gatherings, ask for their prayers, and visit their relics, which often continued to be sources of healing through the Holy Spirit, as during their lifetimes.

In the tenth century, the then-Orthodox Church of Rome began requiring formal recognition of saints by papal authority. The first recorded canonization of this type was St. Ulrich of Augsburg in 993 by Pope John XV. Over the next 600 years, as the Roman Catholic Church separated from the Orthodox community, the West developed a detailed and legalistic method for canonizing saints.

In contrast, the Orthodox Church maintained a more organic approach, similar to early Church practices, where local traditions and practices play a significant role in recognizing saints. The recognition of saints remains a deeply communal and spiritual process, reflecting the continued veneration and local customs of the faithful.

Deacon: For a Christian end to our lives, peaceful, without shame and suffering, and for a good account before the awesome judgment seat of Christ, let us ask the Lord.

Choir: Grant this, O Lord.

Deacon: Remembering our most holy, pure, blessed, and glorious Lady, the Theotokos and ever Virgin Mary, with all the saints, let us commit ourselves and one another and our whole life to Christ our God.

Choir: To You, O Lord.

Notes:

_____
_____
_____
_____
_____

Holy men and women are often recognized for their sanctity during their lifetimes and continue to be honored after their deaths. Christians seek their intercessions and visit their shrines. Saints come from every country and culture, including Greece, Turkey, Russia, Serbia, Romania, America, Palestine, Libya, Egypt, France, Ireland, and Italy. They represent all walks of life: men and women, married couples, royalty, soldiers, merchants, slaves, students, peasants, aristocrats, clergy, monks, and nuns.

These saints were ordinary people who dedicated their lives to God, allowing Him to transform them from within. Regardless of their background, language, or status, they upheld their faith in Christ with honesty and integrity. They exemplified courage, determination, love, humility, grace, and joy. Their lives reveal the highest human potential and serve as role models for us today.

By learning about the saints, we deepen our relationship with their Master and ours, Jesus Christ. Their stories inspire us to live with the same dedication and integrity, showing that holiness is attainable for all who commit their lives to God.

A Complete Guide to The Divine Liturgy

PRAYER OF PREPARATION

(Proskomide)

Priest (*in a low voice*): Lord, God Almighty, You alone are holy *(Rev 15:4)*. You accept a sacrifice of praise *(Heb. 13:15)* from those who call upon You with their whole heart *(Psalm 9:1)*. Receive also the prayer of us sinners and let it reach Your holy altar. Enable us to bring before You gifts and spiritual sacrifices *(Heb 5:1)* for our sins and for the transgressions of the people *(Hebrews 9:7)*. Make us worthy to find grace in Your presence so that our sacrifice may be pleasing to You and that Your good and gracious Spirit may abide with us, with the gifts here presented, and with all Your people.

Priest: Through the mercies of Your only begotten Son with whom You are blessed together with…

Notes:

Peace, Love, Faith

To be worthily present at the celebration of the Holy Mysteries in the Eastern Orthodox Church, several key elements are essential: **peace** of soul, mutual **love**, and the Orthodox (true) **Faith** that unites all believers. Peace of soul involves inner tranquility and freedom from worldly distractions, allowing worshippers to fully focus on the divine. Mutual love emphasizes the importance of harmony and forgiveness among the congregation, reflecting Christ's command to love one another. The Orthodox Faith ensures a shared belief in the teachings and traditions passed down through the centuries.

Following the Litany of Supplication, the priest bestows a blessing upon the people. This blessing signifies God's grace and the spiritual readiness of the congregation to participate in the Holy Mysteries.

The Eastern Orthodox Church places great importance on the communal and mystical aspects of worship. The celebration of the Holy Mysteries, particularly the Divine Liturgy, is seen as a participation in the heavenly worship and a foretaste of the Kingdom of God. The emphasis on peace, love, and faith highlights the transformative power of the Eucharist, which not only unites the faithful with Christ but also with each other.

The priest's blessing is more than a ritual; it is a spiritual affirmation that the congregation is prepared to encounter the divine. This preparation and unity are crucial for experiencing the fullness of the Orthodox Christian faith and for receiving the grace that flows from the Holy Mysteries.

Priest: ... Your all-holy, good, and life-giving Spirit, now and forever and to the ages of ages.

Choir: Amen.

Priest: **Peace** be with all.

Choir: And with your spirit.

Deacon: Let us **love** one another that with one mind we may confess: *(The Priest kisses the holy Gifts saying:)* I love You, Lord, my strength. The Lord is my rock, and my fortress, and my deliverer *(Psalm 18:1-2)*.

Notes:

What is The Creed?

Many of us have cherished memories of our grandparents, and some of us even know stories about our great-grandparents. However, as we look further back, our family history often fades into obscurity. In contrast, the life and significance of Jesus Christ have only grown stronger over time. Even 300 years after His death, people were still martyred for their belief in Him. A pivotal moment occurred on October 28, 312 AD, during the Battle of the Milvian Bridge. The night before the battle, Emperor Constantine had a vision of a cross in the sky and heard the words, "En touto nika" (by this sign, you shall conquer). He instructed his soldiers to mark their shields with the sign of the cross, and the following day, they emerged victorious. This victory granted Constantine control over the Roman Empire. Though Constantine did not immediately convert to Christianity, he recognized the profound significance of Jesus. In 325 AD, he convened the First Ecumenical Council, summoning hundreds of bishops, priests, and deacons to debate the nature of Christ. This council was crucial in defining the Orthodox faith, resulting in the Nicene Creed, which remains a cornerstone of Christian doctrine. The phrase "In wisdom, let us be attentive!" during the Liturgy serves as a reminder to focus on the profound truths of the Orthodox faith, as articulated in the Symbol of Faith (the Creed). This call to attention underscores the enduring legacy and importance of understanding and proclaiming the true nature of Christ.

Choir: Father, Son, and Holy Spirit, Trinity one in essence and undivided.

Deacon: *Guard the doors.* Wisdom. Let us be attentive.

THE CREED (SYMBOL OF FAITH)

Choir: I believe in one God, Father Almighty, Creator of Heaven and earth and of all things visible and invisible.

And in one Lord Jesus Christ, the only begotten Son of God, begotten of the Father before all ages.

Notes:

_____
_____
_____
_____
_____

The future of Christianity was uncertain as two factions clashed: one believed Jesus was a good man but "less than God," while the other asserted that Jesus was "of one essence," or consubstantial, with God and the Holy Spirit. A young deacon named Athanasios (later St. Athanasios) argued for the consubstantial view, while Bishop Arius led the opposing side, even composing rhyming songs to spread his beliefs. During a heated debate, Bishop Nicholas (later St. Nicholas) could no longer tolerate the blasphemy and struck Arius in the face. As a result, Nicholas was jailed, and his bishop's epaulettes were removed. That night, the Virgin Mary and Jesus appeared to Nicholas, restoring his epaulettes. The following day, Constantine and others revealed they had dreamt of the epaulettes being replaced, and upon opening the jail, they found Nicholas wearing them.

This shifted momentum toward those who believed in Jesus' consubstantiality with God. After nearly a month of debate, the side affirming Jesus' equality with God and the Holy Spirit prevailed, leading to the creation of the Nicene Creed, which boldly declared the Christian belief. This is why figures like St. Spyridon, St. Nicholas, St. Athanasios, and St. Constantine are venerated in the Orthodox faith. When Christianity's future was uncertain, and defending the faith could be deadly, these saints risked their lives to interpret, defend, and articulate the essence of Christian belief.

Light of Light, true God of true God, begotten not created, of one essence with the Father through Whom all things were made.

Who for us men and for our salvation came down from Heaven and was incarnate of the Holy Spirit and the Virgin Mary and became man.

He was crucified for us under Pontius Pilate. He suffered and was buried.

And He rose on the third day, according to the Scriptures.

He ascended into heaven and is seated at the right hand of the Father.

Notes:

These spiritual giants form the bedrock of our faith. The Orthodox Church demonstrates its depth by carefully vetting its doctrines. Before formally establishing any doctrine, the Church would wait for a generation to pass, allowing the next leaders to assess whether teachings were divinely inspired or influenced by political trends. For example, in 381 AD, 56 years after the First Ecumenical Council, the Second Ecumenical Council revisited the Nicene Creed. The council made a few adjustments, affirming it as divinely inspired and solidifying it as a cornerstone of Orthodox doctrine. This rigorous process ensured that the Creed, a profound statement of faith, has been professed by millions of Orthodox Christians for over 1,600 years.

Why Catholic?

You might wonder why the term "catholic" appears in the Orthodox service. The word "catholic" means "whole" or "universal" in Greek, reflecting the broad scope of the Church's mission to encompass all believers in Christ. This term was first used in early Christianity to describe the universal nature of the Church, as it was meant to be inclusive of all Christians, not just a specific sect. It is not exclusive to the Roman Catholic Church but signifies the universal aspect of the Christian faith. By proclaiming the Church as "catholic," the Orthodox Church emphasizes its commitment to preserving the fullness of Christian doctrine and tradition across the world. This usage highlights the continuity of the Church's teachings from the early Christian community to today.

And in the Holy Spirit, the Lord, the Creator of life, Who proceeds from the Father *(John 15:26)*, Who together with the Father and the Son is worshipped and glorified, Who spoke through the prophets.

In one, holy, ***catholic,*** and apostolic Church.

I confess one baptism for the forgiveness of sins.

I look for the resurrection of the dead and the life of the age to come. Amen.

Notes:

HOLY ANAPHORA

Anaphora, from the Greek meaning "carrying up" or "offering," refers to a pivotal part of the Divine Liturgy where we present bread and wine to God, asking that they be consecrated. This concept traces its roots back to the Old Testament, where priests offered animal sacrifices as acts of worship. In contrast, our modern offering is a spiritual one, symbolizing the fulfillment of the ancient practice through Christ's sacrifice.

An important aspect of the Anaphora is the act of thanksgiving that precedes the consecration. We begin with the phrase "Let us give thanks to the Lord," mirroring the practice of Jesus, who thanked God before performing miracles.

In John 11:38-44, we see this demonstrated clearly. Before raising Lazarus from the dead, Jesus first prays, "Father, I thank You that You have heard Me. I knew that You always hear Me, but I said this on account of the people standing by, that they may believe that You sent Me." After this expression of gratitude, Jesus calls Lazarus out of the tomb. This sequence underscores that gratitude and acknowledgment of God's power are integral to miraculous acts and divine intervention.

Thus, in the Orthodox tradition, the Anaphora embodies both the ancient practice of offering and the Christian understanding of thanksgiving as essential to experiencing divine grace and transformation.

THE HOLY ANAFORA

Deacon: Let us stand well. Let us stand in awe. Let us be attentive, that we may present the holy offering in peace.

Choir: Mercy and peace, a sacrifice of praise.

Priest: The grace of our Lord Jesus Christ, and the love of God the Father, and the communion of the Holy Spirit, be with all of you *(2 Corinthians 13:13-14)*.

Choir: And with your spirit.

Priest: Let us lift up our hearts. *(Lamentations 3:41)*.

Notes:

WHAT IS WORSHIP? WHY IS IT IMPORTANT?

The English words "worship" and "worth" share the same root, highlighting the profound connection between our highest values and our acts of reverence. In Orthodox Christianity, worship represents the ultimate value of our lives. True worship, as described by Jesus in the Sermon on the Mount, is about placing God and His Kingdom above all else (Matthew 6:33). It involves loving God with all our heart, soul, mind, and strength (Mark 12:30).

Worship transcends attending church on Sundays; it is a way of life enriched by the Liturgy. Orthodox theologians often refer to this as "the liturgy after the Liturgy." Attending the Divine Liturgy offers us a moment to dedicate ourselves to God in gratitude and joy, which renews the gift of the Holy Spirit within us. Through the reception of Christ's body and blood, we are nurtured to become more Christ-like—more loving, compassionate, patient, forgiving, and joyful.

This transformative process is known as theosis, a Greek term meaning "becoming like God." In the Liturgy, we are called to become what we worship. The phrase "Let us lift up our hearts" invites us to be spiritually present before God, while the choir's response, **"We lift them up to the Lord,"** affirms our collective aspiration to connect with Him. Thus, worship is not just an act of reverence but a pathway to spiritual transformation, aligning our lives with the divine example we revere.

Choir: We lift them up to the Lord.

Priest: Let us give thanks to the Lord *(Judith 8:25)*.

Choir: It is proper and right.

Priest (*in a low voice*): **It is proper and right to** sing to You, bless You, praise You, thank You *(cf. 2 Thess 1:3)* and **worship You** in all places of Your dominion *(Psalm 102:22)*; for You are God ineffable, beyond comprehension, invisible, beyond understanding, existing forever and always the same; You and Your only begotten Son and Your Holy Spirit. You brought us into being out of nothing *(cf 2 Macc 7:28)*, and when we fell, You raised us up again. You did not cease doing everything until You led us to heaven and granted us Your kingdom to come.

Notes:

How the Old Testament Prefigures the Divine Liturgy

The Old Testament indeed offers profound prefigurations of the Divine Liturgy found in the New Testament. Just as the New Testament describes Jesus' birth, death, and resurrection, the practice of communion for the remission of sins is also anticipated in the Old Testament.

The prophet Isaiah, writing around 700 years before Christ's birth, provides a vivid vision in Isaiah 6:1-7: "I saw the Lord sitting on a throne, high and lofty; and the hem of His robe filled the temple. Seraphs were in attendance above Him; each had six wings: with two they covered their faces, with two they covered their feet, and with two they flew. And one called to another and said: 'Holy, holy, holy is the Lord of hosts; the whole earth is full of His glory.' The pivots on the thresholds shook at the voices of those who called, and the house filled with smoke. And I said: 'Woe is me! I am lost, for I am a man of unclean lips, and I live among a people of unclean lips; yet my eyes have seen the King, the Lord of hosts!' Then one of the seraphs flew to me, holding a live coal that had been taken from the altar with a pair of tongs. The seraph touched my mouth with it and said: 'Now that this has touched your lips, your guilt has departed and your sin is blotted out.'"

Isaiah's vision reflects several elements present in the Divine Liturgy: the Trinitarian hymn "Holy, Holy, Holy," the use of incense symbolizing prayers rising to God, and the purification symbolized by the live coal touching Isaiah's lips. These elements together foreshadow the transformative experience of partaking in Holy Communion, where believers are spiritually renewed and cleansed.

For all these things we thank You and Your only begotten Son and Your Holy Spirit; for all things that we know and do not know, for blessings seen and unseen that have been bestowed upon us. We also thank You for this liturgy that You are pleased to accept from our hands, even though You are surrounded by thousands of Archangels and tens of thousand *(cf Dan 7:10)* of Angels, by the Cherubim and Seraphim, six winged, many-eyed *(cf Ezekiel 10:12),* soaring with their wings *(Isaiah 6:2)...*

Priest: singing the victory hymn, proclaiming, crying out *(Is 6:3),* and saying: *(cf 1 Pet. 3:22, Col. 1:16, Ezek. 10:8-12, 1 Thess. 4:16.)*

Choir: *Holy, holy, holy, Lord of Sabaoth, Heaven and earth are filled with Your glory (Isaiah 6:3).*

Notes:

Why do Orthodox Christians believe that we truly receive the body and blood of Jesus Christ in communion?

Orthodox Christians firmly believe in the real presence of Christ in the Eucharist because Jesus explicitly stated this in the Gospels. In John 6:51-59, Jesus declared:

"I am the living bread that came down from Heaven. If anyone eats of this bread, he will live forever. This bread is my flesh, which I will give for the life of the world. Unless you eat the flesh of the Son of Man and drink His blood, you have no life in you. Whoever eats my flesh and drinks my blood has eternal life, and I will raise him up at the last day. For my flesh is true food, and my blood is true drink. Whoever eats my flesh and drinks my blood abides in me, and I in him. Just as the living Father sent me and I live because of the Father, so he who feeds on me will live because of me. This is the bread that came down from Heaven. Your forefathers ate manna and are dead; but he who eats this bread will live forever."

Jesus spoke these words during His teaching in the synagogue at Capernaum. The clarity of His message underscores the belief in the true, sacramental presence of Christ in the Eucharist.

Historically, early Church Fathers, including St. Ignatius of Antioch and St. Justin Martyr, affirmed this doctrine. They emphasized that the Eucharist is not merely symbolic but an actual participation in the body and blood of Christ, which is essential for salvation and eternal life. This profound truth remains a cornerstone of Orthodox Christian faith, deeply rooted in the teachings of Christ and the tradition of the early Church.

Choir: Hosanna in the highest. Blessed is He who comes in the name of the Lord *(Ps 118:26)*. Hosanna to God in the highest *(MT 21:9)*.

Priest (*in a low voice*): Together with these blessed powers, merciful Master, we also proclaim and say: You are holy and most holy, You and Your only begotten Son and Your Holy Spirit. You are holy and most holy, and sublime is Your glory. You so loved Your world that You gave Your only begotten Son so that whoever believes in Him should not perish, but have eternal life *(John 3:16)*. He came and fulfilled the divine plan for us. On the night when He was delivered up, or rather when He gave Himself up for the life of the world *(John 6:51)*,

Notes:

_____
_____
_____
_____
_____

"Do This in Remembrance of Me"

The command of Christ to partake of His body and blood for the forgiveness of sins is a cornerstone of Christian faith, rooted in 1 Corinthians 11:23-25: "For I received from the Lord what I also passed on to you: The Lord Jesus, on the night he was betrayed, took bread, and when he had given thanks, he broke it and said, 'This is my body, which is for you; do this in remembrance of me.' In the same way, after supper he took the cup, saying, 'This cup is the new covenant in my blood; do this, whenever you drink it, in remembrance of me.'"

This instruction is pivotal to Jesus' ministry, underscoring His awareness of humanity's need for redemption. By instituting this sacrament on the eve of His crucifixion, He emphasized its central role in Christian life. Jesus did not offer a mere suggestion or symbolic gesture but a definitive command: "Do this in remembrance of me."

The gravity of this command is underscored by the timing; Christ chose His final meal with His disciples to impart this critical instruction. If you were aware of your impending death, you would likely share your most vital lessons with loved ones. Likewise, Jesus' choice to highlight the sacrament on the night before His sacrifice underscores its profound importance.

Orthodox Christians honor this command with reverence and devotion, reflecting the belief that this sacrament is not merely symbolic but a real encounter with Christ's sacrificial love, renewing them spiritually and connecting them to the grace of God.

He took bread in His holy, pure, and blameless hands, gave thanks, blessed, sanctified, broke, and gave it to His holy disciples and apostles, saying:

Priest: Take, eat; this is my body, which is broken for you for the forgiveness of sins *(Matthew 26:26)*.

Choir: Amen.

Priest (in a low voice): Likewise, after supper, He took the cup, saying *(1 Corinthians 11:24)*:

Priest: Drink of it all of you; this is my blood of the New Testament, which is shed for you and for many for the forgiveness of sins *(Matthew 26:28)*.

Choir: Amen.

Notes:

"Without the Shedding of Blood…"

Before Christ's sacrificial death, the forgiveness of sins in the Old Testament was achieved through the ritual sacrifice of animals. These sacrifices, described in Leviticus and other parts of the Torah, involved the shedding of blood as a means of atonement. However, this changed dramatically with the death of Jesus Christ. As St. Paul explains in Hebrews 9:11-14:

"But Christ came as High Priest of the good things to come, by a greater and more perfect tabernacle not made with hands, that is, not of this creation. Not with the blood of goats and calves, but with His own blood He entered the Most Holy Place once for all, having obtained eternal redemption. For if the blood of bulls and goats, and the ashes of a heifer, sprinkling the unclean, sanctifies for the purifying of the flesh, how much more shall the blood of Christ, who through the eternal Spirit offered Himself without spot to God, cleanse your conscience from dead works to serve the living God?"

Christ's sacrifice on the Cross rendered the old system of animal offerings obsolete. Known as the "Lamb of God," Jesus' own blood was shed to provide redemption from sin and eternal life. This act transformed the nature of worship from a ritual involving the shedding of blood to a spiritual offering.

In Orthodox Christianity, this transition is reflected in the Eucharist, where believers partake of Christ's body and blood symbolically, commemorating His ultimate sacrifice. This new covenant emphasizes a profound and direct relationship with God, achieved not through repeated animal sacrifices but through Christ's one-time, all-sufficient sacrifice, which cleanses our consciences and enables a new form of worship.

Priest (in a low voice): Remembering, therefore, this command of the Savior, and all that came to pass for our sake, the cross, the tomb, the resurrection on the third day, the ascension into Heaven, the enthronement at the right hand of the Father, and the second, glorious coming.

Priest: We offer to You these gifts from Your own gifts *(1 Chronicles 29:14)* in all and for all.

Choir: We praise You, we bless You, we give thanks to You, and we pray to You, Lord our God.

(All make a prostration, if it be a weekday, but not if it be a Great Feast of the Lord or the Theotokos).

Priest *(in a low voice)*: Once again we offer to You this spiritual worship **without the shedding of blood,** and we ask, pray, and entreat You: send down Your Holy Spirit upon us and upon these gifts here presented.

Notes:

_____
_____
_____
_____
_____

When Does the Wine and Bread Become the Body and Blood of Christ?

Many parishioners might be uncertain about the precise moment when the bread and wine become the body and blood of Christ during the Divine Liturgy. This transformation, known as the "epiclesis," occurs at a specific point in the service.

During the Divine Liturgy, the priest invokes the Holy Spirit with the prayer, "Send down Your Holy Spirit upon us and upon these gifts here presented... And make this bread the precious Body of Your Christ... And that which is in this cup the precious Blood of Your Christ... Changing them by Your Holy Spirit...." This moment of profound significance is where the transformation is believed to occur.

However, many parishioners might not be fully aware of this critical moment for two main reasons. Firstly, the choir often sings hymns loudly during this part of the service, which can overshadow the priest's quiet prayers. As a result, the invocation of the Holy Spirit may go unnoticed. Secondly, this part of the Liturgy coincides with a time of kneeling and personal prayer, making it easy for attendees to miss the priest's words as they focus on their own prayers.

This moment of consecration is central to Orthodox belief, emphasizing the sacredness of the Eucharist. Understanding the timing and significance of the epiclesis can deepen one's appreciation of the Divine Liturgy and the profound mystery of the sacrament.

> ### Changing Them by Your Holy Spirit
>
> In Orthodox Christianity, the epiclesis, or invocation, is crucial during the Eucharist. This moment involves calling upon the Holy Spirit to sanctify the bread and wine. The epiclesis underscores that the Church's life and actions are powered by the Holy Spirit. The Liturgy is a manifestation of divine activity, where God acts through Christ in the Spirit. As the Church teaches, "Where the Spirit is, there is Christ; and where Christ is, there is the Spirit." This unity highlights the integral role of the Holy Spirit in transforming the elements and the worship itself.

Priest: And make this bread the precious Body of Your Christ. Amen.

Priest: And that which is in this cup the precious Blood of Your Christ. Amen.

Priest: *Changing them by Your Holy Spirit.* Amen. Amen. Amen.

Notes:

_____
_____
_____
_____
_____

What Liturgical Items are Used in the Liturgy?

1. **Holy Chalice:** The cup used to hold the wine that becomes the Blood of Christ.
2. **Discos (Paten):** A round plate used to hold the bread that becomes the Body of Christ.
3. **Asterisk (Star):** A small, star-shaped frame placed over the discos to prevent the veil from touching the bread.
4. **Lance:** A small knife used to cut the bread during the Prothesis (preparation) of the Gifts.
5. **Spoon (Lavida):** Used to distribute the Holy Communion (Body and Blood of Christ) to the faithful.
6. **Zeon:** Hot water added to the chalice before Communion, symbolizing the warmth of the Holy Spirit.
7. **Censer:** A vessel for burning incense, used to symbolize prayers rising to God.
8. **Veils:** Small cloths used to cover the chalice and discos.
9. **Large Veil (Aër):** A large cloth covering the chalice and discos, symbolizing the presence of the Holy Spirit.
10. **Cross:** Used by the priest or bishop to bless the congregation.
11. **Candles:** Carried during processions and used on the altar, symbolizing the light of Christ.
12. **Gospel Book:** The book containing the four Gospels, placed on the altar and read during the Liturgy.
13. **Antimension:** A cloth with relics sewn into it, used on the altar for the celebration of the Liturgy.
14. **Liturgical Fans (Ripidia):** Fans often decorated with icons of angels, used during the Liturgy, especially in processions.

Leadership Structures of the Russian Orthodox Church and ROCOR

The Russian Orthodox Church (ROC) and the Russian Orthodox Church Outside Russia (ROCOR) both follow hierarchical structures that reflect their unique histories and jurisdictions.

The ROC, headquartered in Moscow, is led by the Patriarch of Moscow and All Russia. The Patriarch, elected by the Bishops' Council, is the highest ecclesiastical authority within the Church. Below him are the Holy Synod, which governs the Church's affairs, and various metropolitans and bishops who oversee specific regions. The ROC's administrative structure includes numerous dioceses, each headed by a bishop, and further subdivided into parishes.

The ROCOR, established in 1920 due to political upheaval in Russia, operates independently but maintains close ties with the ROC. Its primary governing body is the Synod of Bishops, led by the First Hierarch, who serves as the presiding bishop. The ROCOR's administrative structure mirrors that of the ROC, with dioceses and parishes managed by bishops and priests respectively. The ROCOR also has its own administrative bodies, such as the Council of Bishops, which provides guidance and decision-making for the Church's activities abroad. Despite their distinct organizational structures, both the ROC and ROCOR emphasize the importance of maintaining Orthodox traditions and unity in faith. Both acknowledge Christ as the ultimate Head of the Church, with ecclesiastical leaders serving in roles that support and guide the faithful in their spiritual journey.

Hymn of the Theotokos

The Orthodox Hymn to the Theotokos, commonly known as the "Hymn of the Theotokos" or "Axion Estin," is a profound expression of veneration towards the Mother of God. Sung during the Divine Liturgy and other services, this hymn underscores the unique role of the Theotokos (God-Bearer) in Orthodox Christian theology.

The hymn's central message is encapsulated in the phrase: "**It is truly right to bless you, Theotokos, ever blessed, most pure, and mother of our God.**" This declaration highlights the Theotokos's unparalleled status as the one who bore Christ, the Son of God, in her womb. By affirming her as "more honorable than the cherubim and more glorious beyond compare than the seraphim," the hymn acknowledges her exceptional sanctity and divine favor.

An interesting aspect of this hymn is its connection to the early Church's struggle with Christological controversies. In the 5th century, the Council of Ephesus (431 AD) affirmed the title "Theotokos" against the Nestorian heresy, which questioned the unity of Christ's divine and human natures. The hymn thus reflects the doctrinal clarity established by the Church, celebrating the Theotokos as the integral link between the divine and human.

The hymn is also a testament to the Orthodox Church's rich tradition of integrating deep theological insights with liturgical practice. It serves as a reminder of the Theotokos's role in the incarnation of Christ and her ongoing intercession for the faithful. As St. Gregory Palamas noted, "The Theotokos is the gateway to the divine and the protector of all who seek her intercession."

Priest: So that they may be to those who partake of them for vigilance of soul, forgiveness of sins, communion of Your Holy Spirit *(2 Corinthians 13:13),* fulfillment of the kingdom of Heaven, confidence before You, and not in judgment or condemnation. Again, we offer this spiritual worship *(Romans 12:1)* for those who rest in the faith: forefathers, fathers, patriarchs, prophets, apostles, preachers, evangelists, martyrs, confessors, ascetics, and for every righteous spirit made perfect in faith *(Hebrews 12:23).*

HYMN TO THE THEOTOKOS

Priest: Especially for our most holy, pure, blessed, and glorious Lady, the Theotokos and ever Virgin Mary.

Notes:

_____
_____
_____
_____
_____

> "Remember also all who have fallen asleep in the hope of resurrection unto eternal life."

The Divine Liturgy extends beyond the present congregation to include those who have passed away. During the service, the priest prays for the deceased, starting with his own family and friends and then including names submitted for the Proskomide. This prayerful remembrance aims to bring the departed into God's presence, invoking the imagery from Psalm 67:1 and Psalm 119:135, which speaks of the "light of Your countenance" shining upon them. If you wish to remember someone who has died, you can provide their name to the priest during the week, and they will be included in these prayers. This practice reflects the Orthodox belief in the ongoing communion of saints, both living and departed.

Why Do We Have Icons of Saints in the Church?

In Orthodox churches, icons of the Saints symbolize God's love and strength manifested through human lives. These holy images offer visual reminders of the exemplary lives that God calls us to emulate. Much like a family photo album preserves memories of loved ones, icons remind us that the Saints are integral members of our Orthodox family. Additionally, during baptism, each person is named after a saint, honoring them and encouraging the baptized to follow the saint's virtuous path. This tradition underscores the connection between the faithful and the Saints, providing both a spiritual legacy and a personal example to aspire to.

Choir: It is truly right to bless you, Theotokos, ever blessed, most pure, and mother of our God. More honorable than the Cherubim, and beyond compare more glorious than the Seraphim, without corruption you gave birth to God the Word. We magnify you, the true Theotokos.

(The priest at this time silently prays first for the departed, and then for the living, saying):

Priest *(in a low voice)*: For Saint John the prophet, forerunner, and baptist; for the holy glorious and most honorable Apostles, for Saints(s) _____ whose memory we commemorate today; and for all Your saints, through whose supplications, O God, bless us. *Remember also all who have fallen asleep in the hope of resurrection unto eternal life.*

(Here the priest commemorates the names of the deceased.)

Notes:

_____
_____
_____
_____
_____

The Church Building or Temple and the People of God

Orthodox Churches are structured into three main areas that in some ways reflect elements of the Old Testament Temple in Jerusalem: the narthex (entryway), the nave (main area), and the altar or sanctuary, which is separated by the iconostasis, or icon "screen." This layout parallels the Jerusalem Temple, where the altar area represents the Holy of Holies, the nave corresponds to the court of the faithful, and the narthex to the court of the Gentiles.

The church is consecrated for worship, symbolizing the intersection of the heavenly and earthly realms during the Divine Liturgy, where believers encounter the divine presence. St. Germanos of Constantinople (d. 760 AD) described the church as "an earthly heaven in which the God of heaven dwells and moves," highlighting its sacred nature.

However, the Church is not just a physical structure; it represents the community of believers who gather in God's name. The term "ekklesia" means those called out of the world by God's Word to form His people. Thus, the Church is a living body of Christians united in faith, receiving the Holy Spirit, and relating to God as their Father. The Scriptures underscore that the Church is both a place of worship and a vibrant community of faith, baptized into Christ and committed to sharing the Gospel.

And grant them rest, our God, where the light of Your face shines *(Psalm 4:6)*. Again, we ask You, Lord, remember all Orthodox bishops who rightly teach the word of Your truth *(2 Timothy 2:15)*, all presbyters, all deacons in the service of Christ, and every one in holy orders. We also offer to You this spiritual worship for the whole world, for the holy, catholic, and apostolic Church, and for those living in purity and holiness. And for all those in public service; permit them, Lord, to serve and govern in peace that through the faithful conduct of their duties we may live peaceful and serene lives in all piety and holiness.

Notes:

"You are a chosen race, a royal priesthood, a holy nation, God's own people, that you may proclaim the wonderful deeds of Him who called you out of darkness into His marvelous light. Once you were no people but now you are God's people" (1 Peter 2:9, 19). "You are fellow citizens with the saints and members of the household of God, built upon the foundation of the prophets and apostles, Christ Jesus Himself being the cornerstone, in whom the whole structure is joined together and grows into a holy temple in the Lord" (Ephesians 2:19-21).

Priest: Above all, remember, Lord, our Archbishop _____ Grant that he may serve Your holy churches in peace. Keep him safe, honorable, and healthy for many years, rightly teaching the word of Your truth *(2 Timothy 2:15)*.

Deacon: Remember also, Lord, those whom each of us calls to mind and all your people.

Choir: And all Your people.

Priest (*in a low voice*): Remember, Lord, the city in which we live, every city and country, and the faithful who dwell in them. Remember, Lord, the travelers, the sick, the suffering, and the captives, granting them protection and salvation.

Notes:

> **"We knew not whether we were in Heaven or on earth…"**
>
> In 863, brothers Cyril and Methodius embarked from Constantinople, one of the five major centers of the early Church, to evangelize the Slavic peoples. At that time, the Slavic language had no written form. Cyril and Methodius created the Glagolitic alphabet, which later evolved into the Cyrillic script, and translated the Bible and the Liturgy into Slavic. Their pioneering work laid the foundation for the Christian Church in Bulgaria, Serbia, and Russia.
>
> By 945 AD, Prince Vladimir of Kiev, seeking a suitable faith for his people, sent envoys to various religious centers to observe their worship practices. Upon experiencing the Divine Liturgy in Constantinople, the envoys reported to Prince Vladimir, saying, "We knew not whether we were in Heaven or on earth, for surely there is no such splendor or beauty anywhere on earth. We cannot describe it to you; we only know that God dwells there among men and that their Service surpasses the worship of all other places."
>
> Impressed by this profound spiritual experience, in 988 AD, Prince Vladimir led his people to the Dnieper River, where they were baptized, marking the beginning of the Russian Orthodox Church. This momentous event established the Orthodox faith in Russia, deeply influencing the region's cultural and spiritual heritage.

Remember, Lord, those who do charitable work, who serve in Your holy churches, and who care for the poor. And send Your mercy upon us all.

Priest: And grant that with one voice and one heart *(Romans 15:15)* we may glorify and praise Your most honored and majestic name, of the Father and the Son and the Holy Spirit, now and forever and to the ages of ages.

Choir: Amen.

Priest: The mercy of our great God and Savior Jesus Christ *(Titus 2:13)* be with all of you.

Choir: And with your spirit.

Notes:

_____
_____
_____
_____
_____

The Gift of the Holy Spirit

Receiving "divine grace and the gift of the Holy Spirit" means that regardless of our background—be it language, ethnicity, or socioeconomic status—God's love transforms us with an inexpressible joy. This divine grace invites us to become like God, reflecting His attributes of goodness, holiness, righteousness, mercy, and compassion. As baptized Christians, we are endowed with the Holy Spirit to cultivate these virtues within us. St. Paul emphasizes this in Galatians 5:22, stating, "The fruit of the Spirit is love, joy, peace, patience, kindness, generosity, faithfulness, gentleness, and self-control." This passage challenges us to reflect on whether these qualities are evident in our lives. Are we embodying love, kindness, and patience? Have we embraced the Holy Spirit's presence so that we may become living icons of God's glory, manifesting His divine attributes in our daily interactions?

What Is the Antimension?

The antimension, meaning "instead of the table," is a rectangular cloth consecrated and signed by the local bishop. It features an image of Christ's body on a burial shroud and the four Evangelists. This cloth signifies the bishop's permission for a community to celebrate the Divine Liturgy and can also serve as a portable altar. Its role is crucial; without the signed antimension, a church cannot lawfully perform the Liturgy.

THE LITANY BEFORE THE LORD'S PRAYER

Deacon: Having remembered all the saints, let us again in peace pray to the Lord.

Choir: Lord, have mercy.

Deacon: For the precious gifts offered and consecrated, let us pray to the Lord.

Choir: Lord, have mercy.

Deacon: That our loving God who has received them at His holy, heavenly, and spiritual altar as an offering of spiritual fragrance, may in return send upon us divine grace and the *gift of the Holy Spirit*, let us pray.

Notes:

_____

_____

_____

_____

_____

Meaning of Orthodoxy

The term "Orthodoxy" translates to "true faith" or "true worship." But why do we hold this belief? What sets us apart from other faiths? To start, if you ask who founded the Orthodox faith, the answer is unequivocally Jesus Christ. After Christ's crucifixion, His disciples gathered in an upper room, filled with fear and uncertainty about the future. Suddenly, "there came a sound from Heaven as of a rushing mighty wind, and it filled all the house where they were sitting. And there appeared unto them cloven tongues like as of fire, and it sat upon each of them. And they were all filled with the Holy Ghost" (Acts 2:1-6).

On that very day, the disciples baptized three thousand people into the faith, marking the inception of Christianity's spread. From that pivotal moment to the present, Orthodoxy maintains a direct and unbroken lineage. The practices observed by the disciples, such as the celebration of communion, recitation of the Lord's Prayer, singing of hymns, recitation of the Creed, and delivering sermons, are the same traditions we uphold today.

Moreover, the priest celebrating the Divine Liturgy in your church today is part of an unbroken chain of ordination that traces back to the apostles in that upper room. This continuity is known as "Apostolic Succession," where each bishop who ordains a priest was himself ordained by a previous bishop, creating an unbroken line back to the dawn of Christianity.

Choir: Lord, have mercy.

Deacon: Having prayed for the unity of ***the faith*** and for the communion of the Holy Spirit, let us commit ourselves, and one another, and our whole life to Christ our God.

Choir: To You, O Lord.

Priest (*in a low voice*): We entrust to You, loving Master, our whole life and hope, and we ask, pray, and entreat: make us worthy to partake of your heavenly and awesome Mysteries from this holy and spiritual Table with a clear conscience; for the remission of sins, forgiveness of transgressions, communion of the Holy Spirit *(2 Corinthians 13:14),*

Notes:

_____
_____
_____
_____
_____

The Lord's Prayer

In just 55 words (58 in Greek), Jesus provided a timeless guide on how to pray. The Lord's Prayer is central, recited during the Divine Liturgy and at every sacrament and service in the Church, guiding the faithful in their spiritual lives.

OUR FATHER WHO ART IN HEAVEN

With the word "**Our**," Jesus emphasizes praying as a community within His Church. Notably, the Lord's Prayer omits "I," "me," "my," and "mine." In the original Greek, "Heavens" is used, highlighting God's greatness beyond the universe. This almighty God desires a personal relationship with each of us, underscoring His transcendent yet intimate nature.

HALLOWED BE THY NAME

"**Hallowed**" is an old English word meaning "to make holy" or "to sanctify." We sanctify God's name by living our lives as true believers, reflecting His holiness.

THY KINGDOM COME

These words should give us pause, as we are praying for the end of the world and the arrival of the four horsemen of the Apocalypse (Revelation 6:1-8). We ask for the Last Judgment (Matthew 25:30-46), the final day when everyone will stand before "the dread judgment seat of Christ" (2 Corinthians 5:10). We will be judged based on our compassion, either entering the kingdom "prepared before the beginning of the world" or "the eternal fire prepared for the devil and his angels" (Matthew 25:34, 41).

inheritance of the kingdom of heaven, confidence before You, and not in judgment or condemnation.

Priest: And make us worthy, Master, with confidence and without fear of condemnation, to dare call You, the heavenly God, FATHER, and to say:

THE LORD'S PRAYER

Choir:
Our Father, who art in heaven:
Hallowed be Thy name. Thy kingdom come. Thy will be done, on earth as it is in Heaven. Give us this day our daily bread; and forgive us our trespasses, as we forgive those who trespass against us; and lead us not into temptation, but deliver us from evil *(Matthew 6: 9-13)*.

Notes:

THY WILL BE DONE ON EARTH AS IT IS IN HEAVEN

True fulfillment comes from doing God's will rather than our own, serving His Kingdom rather than our personal desires. Our lives gain meaning by aligning with God's intentions. The essence of the Christian life is aligning our will with God's will, as true satisfaction is found only in following His path.

GIVE US THIS DAY OUR DAILY BREAD

The saints of the Church interpret this petition in two ways. Firstly, it declares our total dependence on God for daily sustenance, acknowledging that everything we have is His gift. Secondly, it is a prayer for the Bread of Life—the Eucharistic Bread, Christ's Body received in Holy Communion, symbolizing the bread of eternal life (John 6:53-58).

FORGIVE US OUR TRESPASSES AS WE FORGIVE THOSE WHO TRESPASS AGAINST US

Forgiveness is at the heart of the Gospel, yet extending it to those who wrong us can be challenging. In Mark 11:25 and Matthew 6:14, Christ emphasizes that we must be willing to forgive others to receive God's forgiveness. Our ability to forgive comes from knowing that God has already forgiven us (Ephesians 1:7; Colossians 1:14). Jesus teaches that the debt of sin God forgives us is much greater than any debt we might hold against others (Matthew 18:23-35). Thus, understanding our own forgiveness empowers us to forgive others.

Priest: For Yours is the kingdom and the power and the glory *(Mat 6:13)* of the Father and the Son and the Holy Spirit, now and forever and to the ages of ages.

Choir: Amen.

Priest: Peace be with all.

Choir: And with your spirit.

Deacon: Let us bow our heads to the Lord.

Choir: To You, O Lord.

Notes:

AND LEAD US NOT INTO TEMPTATION BUT DELIVER US FROM EVIL

The petition "**Lead us not into temptation**" should not be misunderstood to mean that God tempts us. Scripture is explicit: "No one, when tempted, should say, 'I am being tempted by God'; for God cannot be tempted by evil and He tempts no one. Instead, one is tempted by one's own desire" (James 1:13-14). Rather, we ask God to protect us from life's temptations and guide us away from them. This petition reflects our reliance on God to help us remain steadfast and avoid falling into sin.

A Prayerful Gem

A profound moment occurs when the priest prays, "**Master, guide the course of our life for our benefit according to the need of each of us.**" This prayer is a reminder of the personal care of God, who created the cosmos and watches over all creation. The same God who sacrificed Himself for humanity is intimately involved in guiding our lives, addressing our unique needs. It highlights the intimate relationship between God and each person, showing His desire to lead us according to our specific circumstances and needs.

Priest *(in a low voice)*: We give thanks to You, invisible King *(1 Timothy 1:17)*. By Your infinite power You created all things and by Your great mercy You brought everything from nothing into being *(cf 2 Macc 7:28)*. Master, look down from Heaven upon those who have bowed their heads before You; they have bowed not before flesh and blood but before You the awesome God. Therefore, **Master, guide the course of our life for our benefit according to the need of each of us.** Sail with those who sail, travel with those who travel; and heal the sick, Physician of our souls and bodies.

Priest: By the grace, mercy, and love for us of Your only begotten Son...

Notes:

Eucharistic Living: A Life of Gratitude

The Tradition of the Church describes the Eucharist with rich symbolism and profound significance. Referred to as "the Lord's Supper" (1 Corinthians 11:20) and "the marriage supper of the Lamb" (Revelation 19:9), it represents deep communion with God, transforming us into His children. By partaking of the consecrated bread and wine, we partake in the Body and Blood of Christ, aligning with Old Testament sacrifices. Just as the Paschal lamb's blood saved the Israelites from death in Exodus, Christ's Body and Blood protect and sanctify our hearts.

St. Ignatius of Antioch (c. 115 AD) called it "the medicine of immortality," essential for eternal life, purifying us with divine fire that cleanses our sins. Ultimately, the Eucharist encapsulates the life we are meant to lead in communion with God. Understanding its deep connections to our daily lives helps us live more gratefully, viewing each moment—even the challenging ones—as a divine gift.

with whom You are blessed, together with Your all holy, good, and life-giving Spirit, now and forever and to the ages of ages.

Choir: Amen.

HOLY COMMUNION

Priest (*in a low voice*): Lord Jesus Christ, our God, hear us from Your holy dwelling place and from the glorious throne of Your kingdom. You are enthroned on high with the Father and are also invisibly present among us. Come and sanctify us, and let Your pure Body and precious Blood be given to us by Your mighty hand and through us to all Your people.

Notes:

Holy Gifts for the Holy People of God

Saints are more than the figures depicted in our church icons. According to St. Paul, we are all "called to be saints" (Romans 1:7). The Divine Liturgy addresses us, the gathered faithful, as saints. Just before offering the Eucharist, the deacon and priest intone, **"Let us attend! The holy gifts are for the holy people of God."** This echoes the original Greek, "Proskomen! Ta ayia tois ayiois," meaning "Let us attend! The holy (the consecrated body and blood of Christ) for the saints."

In Greek, "ayios" denotes both "saint" and "holy," underscoring that every Christian is called to holiness. This call to sanctity aligns with Christ's teaching that we should strive to be perfect as our Father in Heaven is perfect (Matthew 5:48). Thus, living a saintly life is integral to God's plan, encouraging us to grow ever more Christ-like. This transformation into holiness is not just an ideal but a divine directive, guiding our spiritual journey and deepening our communion with God.

Deacon: *Let us attend.*

Priest: *The holy Gifts for the holy people of God.*

Choir: One is holy, one is Lord, Jesus Christ, to the glory of God the Father *(Philippians 2:11).* Amen.

THE COMMUNION HYMN

Choir: Praise the Lord from the heavens; praise Him in the highest. Alleluia *(Psalm 148:1)* ***(3x).***

(The Communion Hymn changes according to the Feast Day.)

Notes:

At this moment, the "lamb" is divided into four parts and then further into smaller pieces for distribution during communion, known as the Breaking of the Bread. The central part of the prosphora prepared by the Priest bears the letters:

IC = contraction for Jesus

XC = contraction for Christ

NIKA = conquers

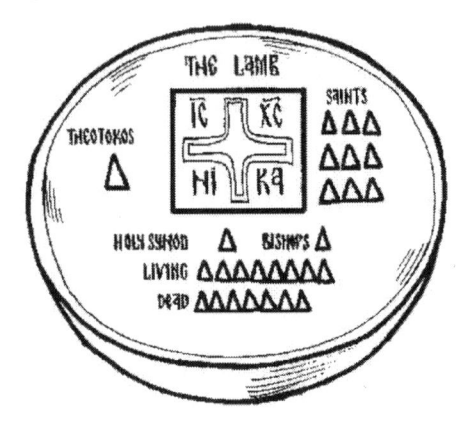

These letters signify:

"Jesus Christ conquers."

The central portion, bearing this inscription and shaped like a cross, is placed on the Diskarion. The priest then breaks this portion into four parts for distribution. This act symbolizes Christ's victory over death and sin.

Priest: The Lamb of God is broken and distributed; broken but not divided. He is forever eaten yet is never consumed, but He sanctifies those who partake of Him.

(Then the priest places the piece that is marked IC into the Holy Chalice saying:)

The fullness of the Cup of Faith, and of the Holy Spirit.

(He then blesses the warm water saying:) Blessed is the ***fervor of Your saints***, now and forever and to the ages of ages. Amen.

Notes:

What is Prosphora?

Prosphora refers to the loaves of bread offered during the Divine Liturgy in the Orthodox Church. Each loaf, called a prosphoron or prosforka in Russian, derives from the Greek word meaning "offering." Typically, Russian Orthodox prosphora are small, about 60mm in diameter, and are made in two parts to symbolize the dual nature of Christ—divine and human. Each loaf is stamped with a seal featuring a cross and the Greek inscription IC-XC NIKA, which translates to "Jesus Christ conquers." In other Orthodox traditions, the loaves are often larger and bear more elaborate seals, reflecting diverse regional practices.

How are Prosphora Used?

Before the Divine Liturgy, the priest selects and prepares five prosphora, or loaves of bread. This is done during a special preparation service known as the prothesis (or proskomedia), conducted quietly within the altar. One prosphora, called the "Lamb," is placed on the Holy Table and, during the Liturgy, is consecrated to become the Body of Christ. When mixed with the consecrated wine, which becomes His Blood, it forms Holy Communion. The remaining four prosphora are used to commemorate the Mother of God, the saints, and both the living and the departed. Additionally, the faithful may offer prosphora on behalf of themselves and their loved ones, living or deceased.

In Russian Orthodox tradition, prosphora are bought at the candle desk near the church entrance.

Names for commemoration are recorded on slips of paper—red for the living and black for the departed—or in a special commemoration book, known as a *pomyanik*. These names are read out during the preparation service and the Divine Liturgy, ensuring that both the living and the deceased are remembered in prayer.

How should the names of those to be commemorated be written?

For commemoration during Orthodox services, use full baptismal names—e.g., Alexander instead of Sasha, and Anastasia instead of Ana. Clergy and monastics should be noted by their full rank—e.g., Reader Michael rather than Michael, Protodeacon Nikolai instead of Father Nikolai, and Abbess Elizaveta rather than Matushka Elizaveta. Avoid including surnames, and ensure names are written clearly and neatly. When writing in Russian, use the genitive case ("родительный падеж"). Only baptized Orthodox Christians may be commemorated during Divine Liturgy. It's essential to check books and lists regularly for accuracy and updates.

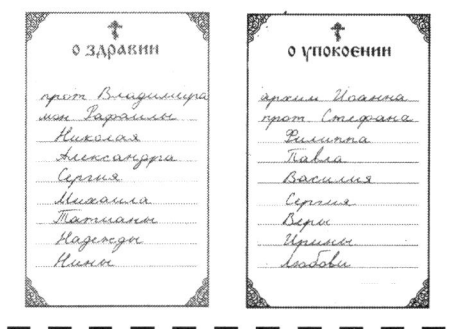

When should prosphora and the lists of names be submitted?

To ensure smooth progress during the Divine Liturgy, prosphora and lists of names should be submitted to the altar well in advance, ideally before the Cherubic Hymn (Херувимская песнь). If prosphora are brought in late, the choir might need to repeat the Cherubic Hymn, causing delays as the priest commemorates late-submitted names. Many parishes allow for ordering prosphora and arranging name commemorations the evening before. Additionally, some parishes set up a system to regularly submit a designated number of prosphora and names at each Divine Liturgy, streamlining the process and ensuring that all requests are handled efficiently.

How are names commemorated by the priest?

The process for commemorating names during Divine Liturgy varies with the number of names. For many names, the priest takes three small particles from each prosphoron, praying for the offerers and those commemorated. The deacon and senior altar servers then read the names. For fewer names, the priest may take a particle for each individual. Afterward, the prosphora are wrapped and returned to the candle-desk for distribution to the offerers. This practice underscores the connection between the Eucharistic celebration and personal remembrance within the Orthodox tradition.

What happens to these particles of bread?

At the end of the Divine Liturgy, the priest or deacon places the commemorative particles into the chalice containing the Body and Blood of Christ. As this is done, the prayer, "Wash away by Thy precious Blood, O Lord, the sins of those commemorated here, through the prayers of Thy Saints," is recited. Alongside these particles, the priest also takes a larger wedge-shaped piece from each prosphoron, known as antidoron, meaning "instead of the gifts." Originally reserved for those who did not receive Holy Communion, antidoron is now distributed to all present as a blessed offering. This practice reflects the Church's emphasis on the communal aspect of the Eucharist.

How should prosphora be eaten?

Prosphora, the blessed bread used in the Divine Liturgy, should be treated with great reverence. It is important to avoid dropping crumbs, which should be collected and either eaten or burned along with the wrapping paper. The paper should be burned rather than discarded in the trash. Children consuming prosphora should be carefully supervised to maintain its sanctity. Traditionally, prosphora is eaten on an empty stomach, often accompanied by Holy Water or a small amount of sweet red wine. This practice reflects the deep respect for the sacred nature of the bread, a tradition rooted in ancient Church customs.

The Fervor of Your Saints....

At this moment in the Divine Liturgy, the priest is presented with a small container of hot water known as "Zeon." This water is blessed and then poured into the Holy Chalice. Symbolically, Zeon reflects the fiery tongues of the Holy Spirit that descended upon the apostles at Pentecost, as described in Acts 2:3. It also represents the blood and water that flowed from Christ's side when pierced by a soldier's lance (John 19:34). Additionally, the priest's prayer highlights that Zeon symbolizes the "fervor" of the saints, embodying their intense devotion and spiritual zeal. This practice connects the Eucharist with profound biblical events and the enduring fervor of the Christian faith.

(*Pouring the water into the Cup crosswise, he says:*) **The warmth of the Holy Spirit. Amen.**

(The Communion Prayers are recited silently by those prepared to receive the holy Mysteries.)

I believe and confess, Lord, that You are truly the Christ, the Son of the living God, who came into the world to save sinners, of whom I am the first. I also believe that this is truly Your pure Body and that this is truly Your precious Blood. Therefore, I pray to You, have mercy upon me, and forgive my transgressions, voluntary and involuntary, in word and deed, known and unknown. And make me worthy without condemnation to partake of Your pure Mysteries for the forgiveness of sins and for life eternal. Amen.

Notes:

Why Do Orthodox Christians Take Communion So Seriously?

The Bible addresses this concern in 1 Corinthians 11, where St. Paul warns: "Therefore, whoever eats the bread or drinks the cup of the Lord in an unworthy manner will be guilty of sinning against the body and blood of the Lord" (1 Corinthians 11:27). Paul advises self-examination before partaking: "A man ought to examine himself before he eats of the bread and drinks of the cup" (1 Corinthians 11:28). He explains that failing to discern the body of the Lord results in judgment, leading to weakness, illness, and even death among believers (1 Corinthians 11:30). Proper self-judgment is crucial, as Paul notes, "But if we judged ourselves, we would not come under judgment" (1 Corinthians 11:31).

How shall I, who am unworthy, enter into the splendor of Your saints? If I dare to enter into the bridal chamber, my clothing will accuse me, since it is not a wedding garment; and being bound up, I shall be cast out by the angels. In Your love, Lord, cleanse my soul and save me.

Loving Master, Lord Jesus Christ, my God, **let not these holy Gifts be to my condemnation** because of my unworthiness, but for the cleansing and sanctification of soul and body and the pledge of the future life and kingdom. It is good for me to cling to God and to place in Him the hope of my salvation.

Notes:

Why do Orthodox Christians Use Incense in Their Worship?

The liturgical use of incense is rooted in biblical instructions and symbolizes sacred practices. According to Exodus 30:1-10, God commanded the creation of an altar for burning incense: "Make an altar of acacia wood for burning incense. It is to be square, a cubit long and a cubit wide, and two cubits high" (Exodus 30:1-2). This altar was to be overlaid with pure gold and placed in front of the curtain before the Ark of the Covenant, where God promised to meet with His people.

Aaron was instructed to burn incense on this altar every morning and evening: "Aaron must burn fragrant incense on the altar every morning when he tends the lamps. He must burn incense again when he lights the lamps at twilight" (Exodus 30:7-8). The incense was made from a specific blend of spices—gum resin, onycha, galbanum, and frankincense—all in equal amounts, and was to be "salted and pure and sacred" (Exodus 30:34). It was considered most holy and should not be replicated for personal use (Exodus 30:37).

In Christian liturgical practice, incense also symbolizes prayer and worship. Revelation 8:3-4 depicts incense in heavenly worship: "Another angel… was given much incense to offer, along with the prayers of all God's people, on the golden altar in front of the throne. The smoke of the incense, together with the prayers of God's people, went up before God from the angel's hand" (Revelation 8:3-4). This connection underscores incense as a symbol of prayer rising to God and emphasizes its ongoing significance in both earthly and heavenly worship.

Receive me today, Son of God, as a partaker of Your mystical Supper. I will not reveal Your mystery to Your adversaries. Nor will I give You a kiss as did Judas. But as the thief I confess to You: Lord, remember me in Your kingdom.

(The Priest prepares to receive Holy Communion.)

Priest: Behold, I approach Christ, our immortal King and God. The precious and most holy Body of our Lord, God, and Savior Jesus Christ is given to me _____ the Priest, for the forgiveness of my sins and eternal life.

Notes:

The Book of Revelation, Chapters 5 and 8

In Revelation 5:6-8 and 8:3-4, the vision of heavenly worship reveals profound symbolism. John describes a Lamb, appearing as though it had been sacrificed, standing at the center of the throne surrounded by the four living creatures and the twenty-four elders (presbyters). The Lamb takes the scroll from the right hand of God, signifying His authority and fulfillment of divine will.

Following this, the four living creatures and the elders fall before the Lamb, each holding a harp and golden bowls filled with incense, which represent "the prayers of the saints" (Revelation 5:8). The incense symbolizes the sacredness of these prayers, ascending to God as an offering of worship.

In a later vision, Revelation 8:3-4 depicts an angel at the altar with a golden censer, presenting "much incense" alongside the prayers of all the saints. The smoke of the incense, mingled with these prayers, rises before God from the angel's hand, illustrating how the prayers of the faithful are cherished and held in reverence in heavenly worship.

This imagery underscores the significance of prayer in Christian spirituality and its role in the eternal divine liturgy. The use of incense as a symbol of prayer highlights its transformative power, bridging the earthly and the divine in worship.

(He then partakes of the sacred Bread.)

The precious and most holy Blood of our Lord, God, and Savior Jesus Christ is given to me _____ the priest, for the forgiveness of my sins and eternal life.

(He then drinks from the Chalice.)

(Afterwards, he wipes the Chalice, kisses it, and says:) This has touched my lips, taking away my transgressions and cleansing my sins.

(The priest then transfers the remaining portions of the consecrated Bread into the Cup, saying:)

Notes:

_____
_____
_____
_____
_____

Who May Receive Holy Communion in the Orthodox Church?

In Orthodox Christianity, full participation in the Divine Liturgy is achieved through receiving Holy Communion, following Christ's command in John 6:53. To partake, one must be a baptized or chrismated Orthodox Christian whose beliefs and actions align with Church teachings. Proper preparation includes a clean conscience, prayer, fasting, and living in charity, aligning with the Apostle Paul's warning in 1 Corinthians 11:27-30 about receiving Communion "in an unworthy manner." Those aware of serious sins should first partake in confession to reconcile with Christ and the Church.

Frequent Communion is encouraged, ideally at every Liturgy. Even young children are invited to receive Communion from infancy, reflecting their parents' faith and following Christ's invitation: "Suffer the little children to come unto Me" (Matthew 19:14). Children under seven typically receive Communion without prior confession, as they are not yet at the age of discernment. This practice underscores the importance of early and frequent participation in the sacrament as integral to Orthodox spiritual life.

Having beheld the resurrection of Christ, let us worship the holy Lord Jesus, the only Sinless One. We venerate Your cross, O Christ, and we praise and glorify Your holy resurrection. You are our God. We know no other than You, and we call upon Your name. Come, all faithful, let us venerate the holy resurrection of Christ. For behold, through the cross joy has come to all the world. Blessing the Lord always, let us praise His resurrection. For enduring the cross for us, He destroyed death by death.

(He takes the holy Cup to the Royal Doors, raises it and says:)

Deacon: Approach with the fear of God, faith, and love.

Notes:

_____
_____
_____
_____
_____

Who Was St. John Chrysostom?

St. John Chrysostom (347-407 AD), the fourth-century Patriarch of Constantinople, stands as a towering figure among the saints and Fathers of the Church. Revered for his dynamic preaching, he earned the title "Chrysostom," meaning "golden-mouthed," due to his exceptional oratory skills. His sermons were so compelling that congregants would often burst into applause. Unflinchingly bold, St. John criticized both political and ecclesiastical corruption and condemned the opulence of the wealthy while advocating tirelessly for the poor. He famously asserted that "feeding the hungry is a greater work than raising the dead," and spearheaded charitable initiatives that provided daily meals to thousands of Constantinople's destitute.

St. John's impact is preserved in over 600 surviving homilies, showcasing his deep commitment to the Scriptures. His commentary on the Acts of the Apostles remains unique as the sole surviving early commentary on this book from the first millennium. He was hailed as "truly evangelical" for his profound scriptural insights. His influential work *On the Priesthood* outlines the virtues and responsibilities required of clergy and continues to be a foundational text in Orthodox seminaries today, shaping the formation of bishops, priests, and deacons.

(*Those prepared come forth with reverence to receive Holy Communion while the people sing the communion hymn.*)

(*When administering Holy Communion, the priest says:*) The servant of God _____ receives the Body and Blood of Christ for forgiveness of sins and eternal life. Amen.

(*When Communion has been given to all, the priest blesses the people with his hand, saying:*)

Priest: O God, save Your people and bless Your inheritance (*Psalm 28:9*).

Notes:

_____
_____
_____
_____
_____

St. John Chrysostom profoundly influenced the Orthodox Liturgy, famously writing that when the priest calls upon the Holy Spirit, "angels attend him and the whole sanctuary is filled with the heavenly hosts." Despite numerous modifications over the centuries, the core of the Eucharistic anaphora, the prayer of thanksgiving and offering, retains its origins from his time. St. John, who passed away in exile in 404 AD due to his outspoken denouncements of imperial excess and clerical corruption, was known for his unwavering faith. His final words, "Glory to God for everything!" reflect his deep spiritual conviction and gratitude even in the face of suffering.

Choir: We have seen the true light; we have received the heavenly Spirit; we have found the true faith, worshiping the undivided Trinity, for the Trinity has saved us.

Priest: *(Having returned the Cup to the holy Table, the priest transfers the particles of the Theotokos and the saints into the Chalice, and then those of the living and the dead saying:)* Wash away, Lord, by Your holy Blood, the sins of all those commemorated through the intercessions of the Theotokos and all Your saints. Amen.

(He covers the vessels and censes them saying:)

Priest: Be exalted, O God, above the heavens. Let Your glory be over all the earth (*Psalm 57:5*)

Notes:

Alleluia! Alleluia! Alleluia!

"Alleluia," an ancient Hebrew expression meaning "Praise God," is a significant term in the Liturgy and is deeply rooted in the Scriptures. It appears extensively in the Book of Psalms, specifically 24 times in Psalms 104, 111-117, and 145-150. The term is also used four times in Revelation 19, where it is the universal cry of joy and adoration for "the wedding of the Lamb" (Revelation 19:7).

In the Orthodox Christian tradition, "Alleluia" is more than just a hymn of praise; it is a central element of the liturgical experience. It is chanted after the Epistle reading, just before the Gospel, during the Great Entrance at the end of the Cherubic Hymn, and as part of the Communion hymn from Psalm 148:1. The term's joyful and spontaneous nature reflects its use throughout the Liturgy to express gratitude and worship.

Notably, "Alleluia" is also a prominent feature during Lent, Holy Week, and even in funerals and memorial services, underscoring its role as a symbol of both celebration and solemnity. Its use in various contexts highlights its versatility and enduring significance in the life of the Church. The tradition of chanting "Alleluia" not only connects worshippers with the historical and spiritual heritage of the Church but also emphasizes a continuous expression of praise and hope in the divine.

(He lifts the vessels and says in a low voice:) Blessed is our God.

Priest *(aloud):* Always, now and forever and to the ages of ages.

Choir: Amen.

Choir: Let our mouths be filled with Your praise *(Psalm 71:8)*, Lord, that we may sing of Your glory. You have made us worthy to partake of Your holy mysteries. Keep us in Your holiness, that all the day long *(Psalm 35:28)* we may meditate upon Your righteousness.

Alleluia. Alleluia. Alleluia.

Notes:

_____
_____
_____
_____
_____

Let Us Attend!

During the Liturgy, it is natural for our minds to wander at times. This is a common experience, and the priest's call to "**Wisdom! Let us attend!**" serves to refocus our attention. This reminder occurs at key moments such as before the Epistle and Gospel readings, the recitation of the Creed, and before the Prayer of Offering, also known as the Anaphora.

Understanding that we are not perfect and our concentration may vary from service to service, it is helpful to view the Liturgy as a multifaceted experience. For those who engage in regular Bible reading, personal prayer, and sincere faith practice, the Liturgy can become a profound source of spiritual nourishment. This depth and richness in the Liturgy are similar to understanding and appreciating a sport: a person unfamiliar with the rules may find it dull, whereas someone well-versed in the game finds it captivating and enriching.

The key to overcoming distractions during the Liturgy lies in diligent spiritual preparation outside of the service. Just as a sports enthusiast studies and practices to gain a deeper appreciation of the game, so too should we invest time in spiritual disciplines—such as prayer, Scripture study, and reflection—during our daily lives. By doing so, we enhance our ability to fully engage with the Liturgy and derive its spiritual benefits. This approach helps transform moments of distraction into opportunities for deeper connection and worship.

PRAYER OF THANKSGIVING

Deacon: *Let us attend.* Having partaken of the divine, holy, pure, immortal, heavenly, life-giving, and awesome Mysteries of Christ, let us worthily give thanks to the Lord.

Choir: Lord, have mercy.

Deacon: Help us, save us, have mercy upon us, and protect us, O God, by Your grace.

Choir: Amen.

Deacon: Having prayed for a perfect, holy, peaceful, and sinless, day, let us commit ourselves, and one another, and our whole life to Christ our God.

Choir: To You, O Lord.

Notes:
_____
_____
_____
_____
_____

Direct Our Ways in The Right Path

It can be deeply disheartening for parishioners to discover that a loved one has drifted away from the faith or stopped attending church. For many, it is particularly painful to see a grandchild or child move away from the spiritual path they once shared. A significant factor in this phenomenon is family involvement in religious practices, especially the role of fathers.

A comprehensive study conducted in the US in the mid-20th Century examined the transmission of faith across generations in the Catholic Church. The research revealed a striking correlation between fathers' church attendance and the likelihood of their children remaining active in the faith. If both parents were engaged in religious practices—attending church, praying, and involving their children—the study found that 80% of their children continued in the faith. In contrast, if only the mother was committed, 35% of the children stayed in the church, and if only the father was involved, the likelihood increased to 50%.

This highlights the profound impact a father's presence and participation in church life can have on a child's spiritual journey. Fathers who attend church with their children not only set a powerful example but also significantly enhance the chances of their children remaining in the faith as they grow older. Encouragingly, this study underscores the importance of active parental involvement in nurturing religious faith. Fathers, by joining your children in worship and spiritual activities, you play a crucial role in fostering their enduring connection to the faith. This commitment is a vital contribution to ensuring that future generations remain anchored in their spiritual heritage.

Priest (*in a low voice*): We thank You, loving Master, benefactor of our souls, that on this day You have made us worthy once again of Your heavenly and immortal Mysteries. *Direct our ways in the right path, establish us firmly in Your fear, guard our lives, and make our endeavors safe*, through the prayers and supplications of the glorious Theotokos and ever Virgin Mary and of all Your saints.

Priest: For You are our sanctification and to You we give glory, to the Father and the Son and the Holy Spirit, now and forever and to the ages of ages.

Choir: Amen.

Notes:

Let Us Depart in Peace

In the early practice of the Divine Liturgy, the words "**let us depart in peace**" marked the conclusion of the service. Over time, however, the dismissal evolved into a more elaborate section known as "The Dismissal." This part incorporates scriptural passages such as Genesis 12:3, Psalm 27:9, Psalm 25:8, and James 1:17, enriching the farewell with profound biblical references. One of the most poignant prayers in this section is directed towards the icon of Christ, where the priest asks for divine blessings, sanctification, protection, and peace, acknowledging that "every good and perfect gift" comes from God. This prayer beautifully encapsulates the essence of the liturgical conclusion. At the Preparation Table, the priest offers a silent prayer, reflecting on Christ's completed work. He proclaims that Christ has fulfilled the prophecies of the Old Testament and accomplished His mission of salvation. He then petitions the Lord to "fill our hearts with joy and gladness" eternally.

The Divine Liturgy concludes with a final prayer, where the priest invokes God's mercy and seeks the intercessions of a wide array of holy figures: the Virgin Mary, the angels, the cross, the apostles, John the Baptist, all martyrs, the church's patron saint, Joachim and Anna, and the saint of the day. This invocation reflects the deep communion with the "cloud of witnesses" that surrounds us (Hebrews 12:1), calling upon the saints to intercede on our behalf—a powerful and unifying moment in the service. During the forty days following Pascha, the dismissal is replaced by the Paschal troparion, proclaiming "Christ is Risen – Truly He is Risen!" This joyful exclamation highlights the celebration of Christ's resurrection, adding a vibrant note to the liturgical conclusion.

PRAYER BEFORE THE AMBO

Priest: *Let us Depart in peace.*

Deacon: Let us pray to the Lord.

Choir: Lord, have mercy.

Priest: Lord, bless those who praise You *(Genesis 12:3)* and sanctify those who trust in You. Save Your people and bless Your inheritance *(Psalm 27:9)*. Protect the whole body of Your Church. Sanctify those who love the beauty of Your house *(Psalm 25:8)*. Glorify them in return by Your divine power, and to not forsake us who hope in You. Grant peace to Your world, to Your churches,

Notes:

_____
_____
_____
_____
_____

Who Are Joachim and Anna?

At the end of the Divine Liturgy, the names Joachim and Anna are mentioned, recognizing them as the parents of the Virgin Mary and, thus, the grandparents of Jesus. Joachim and Anna were deeply devout but struggled with infertility for fifty years. During a visit to Jerusalem to offer sacrifice, Joachim faced scorn from the High Priest Issachar, who derided him for his childless state, and others criticized him as well. Distressed by this, Joachim examined genealogical records and found that every righteous man had been blessed with children—except him.

In response to their profound sorrow, Joachim and Anna prayed fervently, asking God to grant them a child as He had done for Abraham and Sarah. Joachim retreated to a high mountain with his flocks, while Anna prayed in her garden. The Archangel Gabriel then appeared to both, announcing that Anna would bear a daughter destined to bless all nations and bring salvation to the world. Soon after, Anna conceived, and nine months later, she gave birth to the Virgin Mary.

The Church celebrates the Conception of St. Anna on December 9 and the Nativity of the Theotokos on September 8. These feasts honor the miraculous birth of Mary, who would become the Mother of God, and reflect the profound faith and divine intervention that marked her parents' lives.

to the clergy, to those in public service, to the armed forces, and to all Your people. For every good and perfect gift is from above, coming from You, the Father of lights *(James 1:17)*. To You we give glory, thanksgiving, and worship, to the Father and the Son and the Holy Spirit, now and forever and to the ages of ages.

Choir: Amen.

Blessed is the name of the Lord, both now and to the ages (*3x*).

(The priest proceeds to the Prothesis and prays in a low voice:)

Notes:

_____
_____
_____
_____
_____

Sharing His Presence with the World

What is the final act we perform at the Divine Liturgy? It's not the veneration of the cross, the receiving of the antidoron, or the singing of a hymn. The true conclusion of the Liturgy is our departure from the Church. After gathering to be in God's Presence and partaking in the Mystical Supper He provides, we are sent out to carry His Presence into the world.

In essence, this departure transforms us into missionaries of God's Presence and Kingdom. The heart of our evangelical mission is to share the divine gifts we have received. The Divine Liturgy encapsulates our Christian life, empowering us to spread God's love and compassion to a world marred by suffering and sin.

Our mission is to serve others by offering them the communion with the one, true, and living God that we experience in the Liturgy. This act of giving is the ultimate expression of our faith. As we leave the church, we are called to embody and disseminate the transformative grace and peace we have received, thus discovering the true meaning and purpose of our lives. Indeed, the final act of receiving is giving.

Priest: Christ our God, You are the fulfillment of the Law and the Prophets. You have fulfilled all the dispensation of the Father. Fill our hearts with joy and gladness always, now and forever and to the ages of ages. Amen.

Deacon: Let us pray to the Lord.

Choir: Lord, have mercy (*3x*). Father, give the blessing.

Priest: May the blessing of the Lord and His mercy come upon you through His divine grace and love always, now and forever and to the ages of ages.

Choir: Amen.

Notes:

What Is Antidoron?

In the early Christian era, most parishioners received Holy Communion regularly. Over time, however, fewer people participated. To maintain the connection of those not partaking, the Church introduced the "Antidoron," a Greek term meaning "instead of the Gift." This practice involves distributing small pieces of bread at the end of the service, which are cut from the preparation loaves. While not the Body of Christ, the Antidoron is blessed and considered spiritually significant, symbolizing a connection to the Eucharistic celebration.

Dismissal:

At the Dismissal, the priest prays for the intercession of the Theotokos, the saint of the church, the saint of the day, and the righteous ancestors of God, Joachim and Anna, the parents of the Virgin Mary. He asks Christ, our true God, to have mercy on us, acknowledging Him as "good and the Lover of mankind." After this, the priest steps down to the ambo and holds the Holy Cross for the faithful to venerate. He also distributes the antidoron, pieces of prosphora left from the Eucharist. The faithful come forward to kiss the Cross, affirming their faith in Christ, the focus of the Divine Liturgy they have just participated in.

Priest: Glory to You, O God, our hope, glory to you.

Choir: Glory to the Father, and to the Son, and to the Holy Spirit: both now and ever, and unto ages of ages. Amen. Lord, have mercy; Lord, have mercy; Lord, have mercy. Father (Master, *if a bishop is present, whether he serve or not*), bless.

Priest: May Christ our true God (*cf John 17:2*) (who rose from the dead), as a good, loving, and merciful God, have mercy upon us and save us, through the intercessions of His most pure and holy Mother; *(and the rest)* of our father among the saints, John Chrysostom, Archbishop of Constantinople; (*and of the saint(s) whose temple it is and whose day it is*); of the holy and Righteous Ancestors of God, Joachim and Anna; and of all the saints: have mercy on us and save us, for He is good and the Lover of mankind.

Choir: Amen. The Orthodox episcopate of the Russian Church; our Lord the Very Most Reverend Metropolitan _____, First Hierarch of the Russian Church Abroad; and our lord the Most Reverend Bishop _____; the brotherhood of this holy temple, and all Orthodox Christians: preserve, O Lord, for many years!

Priest: Through the prayers of our holy fathers, Lord Jesus Christ, our God, have mercy on us and save us.

Choir: Amen.

Priest (*blessing the people*): May the holy Trinity protect all of you.

> At this point, the priest may serve a moleben, if he wishes. The cross is then venerated by the faithful who have not received the Holy Mysteries, and the antidoron is distributed. Those who have communed venerate the cross after the Thanksgiving prayers.

Notes:

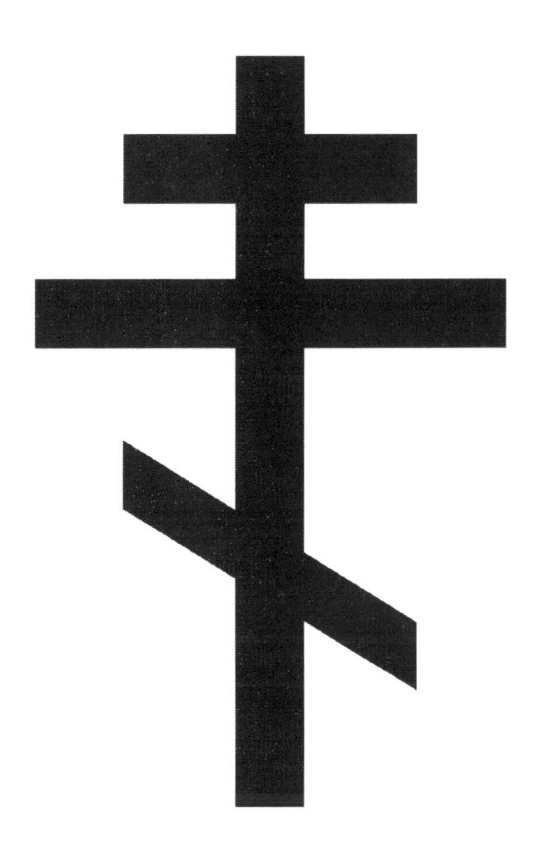

REFERENCES & SOURCES

Gogol, N. (2014). *Meditations on the Divine Liturgy.* Printshop of St Job of Pochaev.

Holy Trinity Monastery. (2022). The divine liturgy of our father among the Saints John Chrysostom: Slavonic-English parallel text. Holy Trinity Publications.

Made in the USA
Las Vegas, NV
18 February 2025

18330670R10098